# BIG IMPACT
## LANDSCAPING

# BIG IMPACT
# LANDSCAPING

## 28 DIY PROJECTS YOU CAN DO ON A BUDGET TO BEAUTIFY AND ADD VALUE TO YOUR HOME

## SARA BENDRICK

LANDSCAPE DESIGNER & CONTRACTOR, HOST OF DIY NETWORK'S *I HATE MY YARD!*

PAGE STREET
PUBLISHING CO.

PAGE STREET
PUBLISHING CO.

First published in 2017 by
Page Street Publishing Co.
27 Congress Street, Suite 105
Salem, MA  01970
www.pagestreetpublishing.com

Distributed by Macmillan, sales in Canada by The Canadian Manda Group.

21   20   19   18   17        1   2   3   4   5

ISBN-13: 978-1-62414-339-7
ISBN-10: 1-62414-339-3

Library of Congress Control Number: 2016963758

Cover and book design by Page Street Publishing Co.
Photography by Joe Dodd; except by Dylan Eastman on pages 15 (left), 36 (top), 46 (middle), 52 (right), 54, 56, 57 (bottom middle), 58 (top), 60 (right), 72 (right), 73 (middle), 76 (top  middle), 77 (bottom), 96, 98 (top), 106, 108 (top), 118, 119 (bottom middle), 124 (bottom middle), 151 (left and bottom and middle top right), 152 (top and bottom), 167, 170 (bottom), 172, 173, and 181 (right); Shutterstock on pages 13, 15 (right), 16 (bottom), 17 (middle and bottom), 18 (top, bottom middle and bottom), 33 (top and bottom), 44, 51, 52 (left), 57 (top), 58 (middle and bottom), 60 (left), 72 (left), 74, 75 (top, top middle, bottom middle and bottom), 77 (middle), 91 (top), 97, 98 (bottom and middle), 99, 100, 101, 110–113, 121–123, 124 (top, bottom middle and bottom), 125 (middle and bottom), 131 (right), 132, 134, 137 (bottom), 139, 140 (left), 141, 142, 144, 151 (top), 152 (top middle), 164 (bottom and middle), 175 and 179 (bottom); Grant Sukchindasathien on page 50; and Jessica Diaz on page 182.
Drawings by Sara Bendrick

Printed and bound in the Unites States

Page Street is proud to be a member of 1% for the Planet. Members donate one percent of their sales to one or more of the over 1,500 environmental and sustainability charities across the globe who participate in this program.

## DEDICATION

I WOULD LIKE TO DEDICATE THIS
BOOK TO MY FAMILY, WHO HAVE ALWAYS
SUPPORTED MY CREATIVE ENDEAVORS

# CONTENTS

# INTRODUCTION

Whether this book was given to you as a gift or you purchased it for yourself, I have to assume that you are curious and handy . . . or you want to be. I have to assume you are driven, as most DIYers are. My hat's off to you and the many projects you dream up for your exterior space.

Spending time outdoors is one of the easiest and most fulfilling ways to improve your quality of life. I hope you find inspiration in these pages and I can't tell you how grateful I am for your interest in my projects and ideas. From a crafty little girl to a starving college student to a landscape contractor, I have found many opportunities to do what I love, and luckily, most of the time I get paid to do it!

I have been involved in the world of exterior design, construction and maintenance for almost ten years. One of my first hands-on jobs in the landscape industry was as a landscape forewoman running a maintenance crew for an apartment complex and all the city's libraries. It was not a glamorous job—imagine directing a motley crew of non-English-speaking hardworking laborers and ex-convicts from employment agencies. I ran the scheduling and worked side by side while we trimmed, hedged, mowed and emptied the trash from all the city libraries (to be honest, public trash is no joke: that stuff is pretty gross!). But I'm glad I had the job, and I'm glad I had a boss who wasn't afraid to let me take a stab at doing what some people might consider an unconventional job for a female college student. I learned a ton, and I was blissfully unaware of the stereotypes and limits that other people may have set for me; for that I am grateful.

After graduating with a bachelor's degree in landscape architecture from California Polytechnic–San Luis Obispo, I found myself working for a residential design-build company. I learned to love residential design and working with individuals. People's homes are a reflection of who they are and what they love, and it's very satisfying to be able to guide my clients in designing functional and relaxing environments that they will experience every day.

In 2012 I received an email stating that the DIY Network was looking for a landscape expert to host a landscaping show. I sent in an email with a brief introduction, a portfolio of my work and a photo. Within three weeks of reaching out, I beat out almost two thousand applicants and got the position! Around the same time, I started Sarita Landscape Design, a residential company named after my grandpa's nickname for me, Sarita, which means "Little Sara" in Spanish.

Since then, I have secured an active landscape contracting license and I balance landscape design, contracting and TV/media engagements. With DIY Network's *I Hate My Yard!* under my belt and a new series, *Build It Like Bendrick*, in the works, I am keeping myself out of trouble.

It has always been my dream to write a book that gives an inside view of landscape materials and projects that can affect the overall function or aesthetic of a home. On a daily basis I am explaining landscape processes and ideas to clients, from DIYers to DIFMers ("do-it-for-me"-ers). In this book you will learn how to start making educated decisions based on your budget and your style. You will also find some instructional projects of various skill levels: beginner, intermediate and advanced. You can customize projects to fit your situation or simply to understand the principles of how these projects come together.

Cost is taken into consideration for all of the projects presented in this book. Because prices will vary from region to region, depending on the level of customizing and sizing, the following key gives a rough estimate of what to expect.

$ = INEXPENSIVE, MINIMAL COST
$$ = REASONABLY INEXPENSIVE
$$$ = EXPENSIVE
$$$$ = VERY EXPENSIVE

* Time given for these projects is approximate and is assuming you have two to four sets of hands to help move things along for the bigger projects. If you are working solo, expect the projects to take at least twice as long. Working with a buddy or two really does keep things rolling. Plus, it's a lot more fun that way.

Thank you for picking up this book and supporting my journey. I hope it is a resource you will turn to again and again as a guide for your own projects.

# LIVING LA VIDA OUTSIDE

## OUTDOOR LIVING ELEMENTS THAT CHANGE WHERE YOU SPEND YOUR TIME

I take any chance I can get to be outside, whether it's for work, to dine, to play or to relax. I always feel more alive after spending time walking under trees or relaxing in the sunshine. We should all welcome opportunities for comfortable outdoor experiences, as they elevate our moods and clear our minds. This section focuses on how outdoor living spaces can enhance your home and the various elements you can build to bring you and your family outside more often to make the most of your yard.

## OUTDOOR LIVING

Did you know that scientists from the University of Illinois and the University of Hong Kong, along with other researchers, have found that looking at trees significantly reduces stress in as little as five minutes? That is pretty incredible considering how simple it is. There are numerous studies that link exposure to nature with lower stress, faster healing and improved overall health. I've never had a client who regretted adding an outdoor kitchen or living area.

An outdoor living space can be one of the most significant areas of your home. Nothing makes our hearts more content than relaxing in dappled sunlight with a warm summer breeze wafting over us. We have the power to manipulate our surroundings in a manner that benefits our entire family. This is quite amazing if you think about it: we can make an environment of our own design!

So what is an outdoor living room? It is any space that is created with the intention of outdoor living, such as a dining area, a lounging area, a kitchen area or a combination of any or all of these. An outdoor space can have not only a functional living area but also a quiet beauty that serves your needs for a long time to come. Unlike a room addition, creating entertaining or lounging areas outside offers a completely different aesthetic and purpose. An open-air room allows you to experience the outdoors by bringing comfortable living elements outside.

It's important to figure out your priorities when tackling a job. Know how you want your space to feel and how you want it to function. Those priorities will guide the direction of a renovation. Depending on where you live, you may need to consider climate factors. Hot climates have different issues to consider than colder climates. But despite your climate, elements such as outdoor heaters or fire features for cold evenings, misters for hot climates, lighting for evening use and shade structures for hot areas can maximize your enjoyment of outdoor living spaces and extend their usefulness. Allow your imagination free reign; there are always new and creative possibilities to explore.

## ENHANCING PROPERTY VALUE

Landscaping and building structures can be expensive, so should you expect your property value to increase because of the large investment you're making? To keep it simple . . . it depends. There are many factors that affect the value of a property, from ZIP code to local neighborhoods to the current economy.

To truly determine whether a project is a good idea in terms of return on investment, you need to rely on your local realtors and appraisers for valuable information about your local market. This is the most accurate way to determine whether you will see a return on investment (ROI). In my opinion, it's a good idea to have the mind-set that you're renovating in order to enhance your quality of life and functional living space for you and your loved ones first, and that an ROI is simply an added bonus.

If you live in a neighborhood where all the homes have shade structures, pools and fire pits and your property doesn't, then expect your unimproved property to sell at a lower price. If you spend as much as $50,000 to $100,00 to catch up to the neighborhood, you will likely increase to the market price of your neighborhood, but you also most likely won't see a 100 percent ROI. Also, if your neighbors haven't installed patios and pools and so on, and you plan to, keep in mind that your home value will likely increase, but not significantly more than the average home in your neighborhood. It's best to check with your local real estate professionals if ROI is a concern for you.

## POPULAR OUTDOOR LIVING ELEMENTS

When it comes to outdoor living, there are countless options, depending on your space, your style and your needs. Thinking of the opportunities can be exciting! Imagine lounging in a nice comfortable sofa chair with a glass of white wine and the aroma of marinated vegetables on the grill wafting your way. Achieving such a space can mean anything from purchasing furniture and a grill to custom building a space to the exact dimensions of your yard.

Popular exterior features to consider include kitchens, bar counters and grills (Chapter 1); fire features such as fireplaces and fire pits (Chapter 2); water features such as fountains (Chapter 3); overhead structures such as pergolas and arbors (Chapter 4); and space for outdoor games such as a bocce court (Chapter 5). Section Two offers an in-depth understanding of "hardscape" materials: stone, lumber, metal and masonry (Chapters 6–9), and Section Three introduces "softscape" topics: soil building, plantings, gardens, décor and lighting (Chapters 10–13). Of course, most of us would love to have them all, but space, time and budget may be limiting factors. So planning, phasing or value engineering are valuable options. Inviting family and friends to enjoy your yard and try out all the amenities may be the most important element of all.

Most of your money will be spent investing in outdoor living elements, whether you do it yourself or hire it out. Consider your key features carefully. Ask yourself, "How do I like to entertain?" "How many people do I want to gather in an area?" and "Do I want a relaxing and intimate setting or a social and fun environment?"

# CHAPTER I

# OUTDOOR KITCHENS AND BARS

## THE MODERN-DAY WATERING HOLE

If your family is like mine, we all hover around the place where the food is being cooked. Having an outdoor counter space to prepare meals and drinks, a place to grill and a comfortable seating area will never go out of style. But what makes one kitchen better than another? Ultimately, it comes down to preference and functionality. This chapter will help you sort out the options in order to make the best decision for your home. Various building methods, choices of materials and amenities, and site selection will all be explored, as well as considerations such as adding countertops, a bar and a pizza oven.

Some projects will require professionals, but there are still many roles you can fill by yourself to bring style and functionality to your outdoor space. Built-in counters can quickly get expensive, so the Grill Counter Island project (page 20) will help you cut down on costs and beautify your space with customizable options. And if you like to entertain, you'll love the Swinging Bar Shelf (page 26) project that provides guests with a relaxing place to hang out.

## CONSTRUCTION OPTIONS AND OTHER CONSIDERATIONS

**Permanent kitchen counters** are the ideal choice in my opinion because they can be customized to the location and personal taste. There are a few popular ways to construct a permanent counter. The most common options are building them out of concrete masonry units (CMU), bricks/blocks, steel stud frames and prefab boxes (see the project on page 20 for a grill counter). The benefits of building a solid counter unit are that it is a permanent fixture in your yard, adds value and purpose to a space and is relatively low maintenance.

**Build-arounds** are another option if you are looking to spruce up a nice freestanding grill you already own. You can build counters around the grill with paver blocks or lumber to elevate your existing grill from a stand-alone unit to a built-in look. This typically costs less and is a little simpler than permanent structures.

**Prefabricated grill islands** are usually made from steel stud construction to create a mobile grill unit with counters already built in. These are obviously the simplest way to get a built-in counter as all you need to do is wheel it into place. They function well, but you may lose the ability to customize it and match it to your space.

## LOCATION

Location is probably the most important consideration when designing a kitchen, because once it's built, you can't move it! Typically you want to choose a spot close to your indoor kitchen so that you can easily transfer food and entertainment items. If you have to walk too far—for example, more than 30 feet—to get to your outdoor cooking area, you will use it a lot less. The idea is to extend your indoor living experience, so having close, functional access to your grill setup will increase your usage.

You also want to keep your grill away from flammable materials, so locate it a fair distance away from any wood shingling or flammable surfaces. Some localities require a 10-foot clearance from such surfaces. If you want to place your grill under an overhead structure, you need to check with your local code for height requirements and consider installing a range hood.

## AMENITIES

Amenities are what make your outdoor kitchen customized to your taste. When deciding which features to select for your kitchen, start with the basics. A grill and counter space for preparing and serving are the bare minimum but are still enough to create a great area. There are so many other frills you can add to enhance your kitchen, such as an outdoor fridge, sink, side burners and beer taps, and so on. The options are limited only by your creativity (and, okay, maybe your budget, too!).

## UTILITIES

**Gas.** It's extremely important to consider the utilities when building your structure. How hard will it be to pull your gas line? Do you need to break through 30 feet of concrete to run it? The answers may prompt you to install a grill that runs on a propane tank rather than on a gas line. Get a quote from a licensed plumber or your contractor to help navigate these options.

**Electricity.** Electrical outlets are the second most popular amenity after a gas line because they are versatile and allow you to plug in a fridge or a wine cooler or simply charge your phone.

**Water and sewer.** If you plan on having an outdoor sink, you will need to run water and probably have to tie into a cleanout. Check your local code to see what is required; many areas specify that the spent water be run into the sewer line because they want to protect the environment from contaminants. However, some areas allow you to run cold water into a French drain or other drainage system. If you're putting in a garbage disposal, then you will definitely be connecting to the sewer. All of these features give you a premium, turnkey system, but the more amenities you build in, the pricier it all gets.

## NATURAL GAS VERSUS PROPANE

Most built-in grills use natural gas or propane. Running a natural gas line is more expensive because it usually needs to be buried at least 8 to 24 inches deep, depending on local code, but once it's in, you're done. Using propane tanks for fuel can save money but you have the inconvenience of making sure there is a filled tank on hand or within a quick car trip.

## OPTIONS FOR GRILL UNITS

When it comes to picking out a grill for your outdoor kitchen, you need to look beyond the grill's pretty cover and understand the different materials used to build it to learn what best fits your preferences and your location.

There is a lot of competition in the grill market, and there are many different types of grills and cooking styles—from charcoal to propane to natural gas—and all at different price points. However, you can cook a perfect steak on an affordable grill or burn a steak on a premium grill. Successful grilling comes down to the skill and knowledge of the chef, understanding how the grill cooks and knowing what to expect maintenance-wise. It can be a little overwhelming if you are not a practiced grill chef. But if you begin with what is most important to you, it becomes easier to pick the right grill for your situation.

Things to consider when choosing your grill are maintenance, ease of use, cost and fuel source. You'll also need to select the components that are important to you.

## GRILL HOODS

The grill hood is the shell of the grill that everyone will see, so choose something that ties in with the counter materials and the architecture of the space and will stand up to your natural environment. Below are the most available options.

**Stainless.** Stainless steel grills are popular because they are attractive and contemporary looking. The best-grade stainless steel for hoods is 304 for beauty and durability, and 443 or 316 (marine grade) for resistance to corrosion, which is vital to consider if you live near water. In addition, 430 is a popular stainless steel; although not nearly as durable as 304, it drops the price point while still achieving the stainless steel look. Many lower- to mid-range grills are made from 430. Because it's a lower grade of stainless it is more susceptible to tarnishing and rust over time. You can sometimes pick out a 430 steel grill as they are for bent and screwed units rather than welded, as 430 doesn't weld as well. You'll also need a soft cover for your grill if you are under a tree or near the water to provide protection from tree stains and saltwater corrosion. Even though it's called stainless, it's really *stain resistant*, but that term doesn't have quite the same ring.

### THE MAGNET TEST

Want to make sure you're actually getting top-end 304 stainless? A good way to tell the quality of stainless 304 is with a magnet. A true 304 stainless is barely magnetic.

**Porcelain enamel.** This material is a solid choice because it won't rust unless the enamel or paint chips off. Porcelain enamel is made by bonding a glass finish to metal. It is very durable and rust resistant and has a nice finished look. It's easy to clean and costs less in general compared to quality stainless. On the downside, if porcelain cools down too quickly it can get hairline cracks that may eventually rust.

**Cast aluminum.** Cast aluminum is very durable and its powder-coated layer protects against rust. Typically, this is the finish on affordable short-lived units, but there are a few high-end brands that use cast aluminum. If it ever chips, just repaint it with a high-heat paint, found at any hardware or paint store.

**Ceramic.** Ceramic is an essential part of a kamado-style grill, the most popular of which is the "egg." This style of grill is favored by extreme outdoor grilling enthusiasts because of its versatility—it can grill, smoke and even cook pizzas—and is perfect for people looking to step up their barbecue game.

### COOKING GRATES

The options for cooking grates come down to personal preference, price point and maintenance requirements. One is not better than another—simply different (though some passionate grill chefs may argue for one type over another).

**Stainless steel.** This material is going to cost you more but will hold up to the elements better than cast iron and is easier to maintain. Stainless will not get as hot as cast iron and distributes thermal mass more evenly, providing a more consistent temperature.

**Cast iron.** Because iron is corrosive, cast-iron grates are usually coated with a porcelain enamel or powder-coated finish to protect them from rust. Cast iron will heat up and cool down quicker than stainless and is a bit more work in terms of maintenance. Typically, it is also less expensive, and some people prefer it. Noncoated cast iron is also an option, but you will have to replace these grates more often. Both types of cast iron are more difficult to clean than stainless steel.

## COUNTERS, BARS AND PIZZA OVENS

Counters are probably one of the most popular items people request when looking to cook and entertain outside. From block to concrete to brick and more, the base structure is just the beginning; you also need to decide on the countertop and veneers and whether you want to install appliances or other features.

Outdoor bars are a great addition to any kitchen, especially if you like to keep your guests and yourself hydrated. They are always a popular place to congregate and make beautiful and dynamic backdrops, adding a lot of style to a space. Imagine being outside and having a complete drinks setup, with no bouncing in and out of the house to keep the party going.

A bar makes sense if you plan on entertaining often. You can place it near the outdoor kitchen or dining area and treat the bar like the focal point or tie it into another feature. An outdoor bar can be simple, such as adding a bar shelf or cabinet to make use of vertical space and bring more interest to your outdoor area (see page 26). A mid-range option might be to incorporate outdoor fridges and other bar elements into an existing countertop; or a complex project might be to build a separate unit altogether, so long as it is protected from the weather.

The biggest problems with keeping drinks outside are temperature fluctuations and direct sunlight, which can be mitigated with overhead coverage or cabinets and outdoor wine or beer fridges. Less permanent options include coolers or other decor items that can be used to "dress" the site and set the mood for the evening.

Pizza ovens are another great addition to outdoor kitchens and can be easily added to any countertop or installed as a freestanding unit. Pizza ovens are typically "black ovens," meaning the food is cooked in the same chamber as the fire. The fire is usually pushed to one side and the pizza is cooked at very high heat (650°F to 750°F for a short time, about three minutes). I love incorporating pizza ovens above fireplaces or as built-ins. This is probably the most expensive and also the most effective addition because it becomes a permanent part of the yard as well as a focal piece. However, you don't have to spend big bucks to reap the benefits of a wood-burning pizza oven, as they come in many price ranges and styles. For pizza ovens made from cob or adobe, the cost is minimal but the labor is fairly involved. Most standard prefabricated ovens made from clay or metal cost anywhere from $1,000 to $5,000 or more, ranging from simple to premium models.

## CREATE AN OUTDOOR DINING AREA

An outdoor dining area doesn't have to be overthought: with just a few purchased items you can put together a space with minimal DIY skills. To create this area, I hung iron glass star lantern lights from the tree canopy at different heights to add charm and illumination. Then I rolled out a large 11×9-foot outdoor rug on top of compacted base material to provide a flat, well-draining surface and add a pop of color. Select a dining table that suits your style and fits your family; you can find outdoor furniture at a local furniture or hardware store or online; I bought this nine-piece set online.

# GRILL COUNTER ISLAND

### LEVEL: INTERMEDIATE TO ADVANCED
### COST: $$$
### TIME COMMITMENT: 2–4 WEEKENDS, PLUS MORE TIME TO FINISH
### PROFESSIONALS NEEDED: PLUMBER (FOR GAS LINE, IF USING, AND PERHAPS WATER AND SEWER TIE-INS), ELECTRICIAN (IF RUNNING ELECTRICAL)
### DIMENSIONS: 102" × 102" L-SHAPE

Building a permanent outdoor counter space creates a big-impact, functional area that is bound to be a popular gathering spot. Although classic masonry counters, made out of CMU blocks, rebar, mortar and footings, are within the realm of DIYers, they can be complicated and take a long time to build, especially if you're new to construction projects. I am a big fan of prefabricated cabinet units because they simplify the process and speed up the build. Plus, once you have the units installed, you can choose whatever finish you like, such as stucco, stone veneer or tile, making the prefab structures very versatile and customizable to your style and environment. This project is designed to be placed on a concrete pad. If your selected location does not have a concrete pad, you'll need to hire a mason to pour a 4-inch concrete base that is 2 inches wider or more on all sides of your planned installation. If you're in a climate where the ground doesn't freeze and thaw, you can save time and money by placing the island on 4 inches of compacted base material.

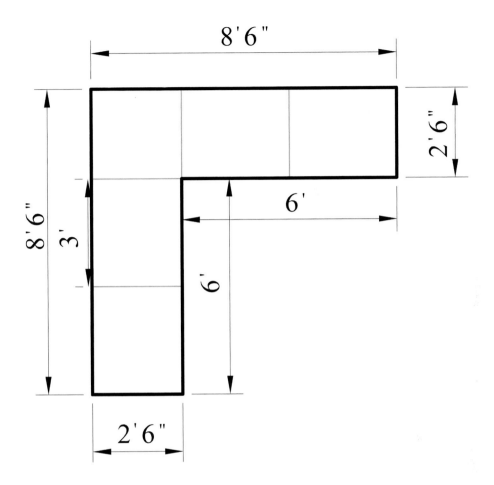

## TOOLS

- Safety gloves
- Square
- String line and stake
- 2'-3' level
- Crescent wrench and socket set
- Pencil
- Tape measure
- Angle grinder with diamond blade
- Triangle or straightedge
- Grinder, wet saw or mason's hammer
- 5-gallon buckets
- Square or triangle trowel
- Rubber mallet
- Torpedo level (mini level)

## MATERIALS

- One corner cabinet, 36" high × 30" long × 30" wide
- Four linear cabinets, 36" high × 36" long × 30" wide
- Two cabinet end caps, 24" high × 24" wide
- Two 10-oz bottles of construction adhesive
- Sixteen galvanized steel fastener sets (1 bolt, 2 washers and 1 nut)
- Plastic shims
- Grill unit
- Finishes of choice for the cabinets (I used stone veneer)
- 27 sq ft of 1" natural flagstone for the counter
- Three 94-lb bags of type S mortar
- One 50-lb bag of thinset

STEP 1: **Choose your location and set a concrete base:** Select a place that has a concrete pad or have one poured. Try to anchor your yard: whether the grill counter will fit into a corner or you create your own "room" with the perimeter of the unit, place it in an area that's easy to get to and close to your other amenities. You will need to hire a licensed plumber to pull a gas line to the area unless you plan on using a propane tank. To help save costs you can do some of the grunt work and dig a trench 20 inches deep (or as deep as local code requires) so the plumber only has to run the line. Consider running other utilities at this time as well, such as water, sewer tie-ins and electrical, depending on what amenities you choose. For this project, we ran the gas line and electrical and located them so that they would sit inside the units.

STEP 2: **Place the cabinet units:** Grab a partner or two to help move the cabinets roughly into place one by one. Use a square or a string line if needed to make sure you align them to each other and parallel to the structure if applicable. Do not push them into place as this can cause hairline cracks.

STEP 3: **Glue the cabinet units together:** Run a line of construction adhesive along the face before you set the next cabinet. The glue can be loose and random. You don't need a lot, as construction adhesive is very strong and is a secondary reinforcement to the bolts. Finally, attach the end caps with the construction adhesive.

STEP 4: **Check the level:** While the adhesive is still workable, place the cabinets together and loosely place the bolts in the predrilled holes. Check your level and make sure they are plumb.

STEP 5: **Bolt the cabinets together:** Use a crescent wrench to secure the bolts and washers in each of the predrilled holes.

**STANDARD HEIGHTS**
Tabletop height: 30 inches
Benches and chairs: 16–18 inches
Standard counter: 36 inches
Bar counter (for use with stools): 40–42 inches
Stools: 28–30 inches

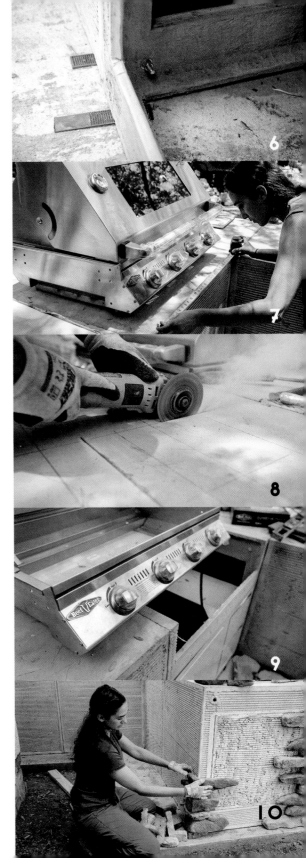

**STEP 6:** **Add shims, if needed:** Now that your cabinets are secure, check your level again. If needed, use shims to adjust the level. Be sure to use plastic shims because they will not rot over time the way wood does, which can cause shifting.

**STEP 7:** **Measure and mark:** Use a pencil and tape measure to mark out the footprint of the grill and other appliances that need to be inset. Most manufacturers will also give "cut out" recommendations for their unit if you don't trust your measuring skills or are unsure of what to measure to be cut.

**STEP 8:** **Cut out the grill's footprint:** Use an angle grinder with a diamond blade to cut out the area for your barbecue and other amenities. This tool is very effective but can be dangerous if not handled correctly. I don't recommend this tool for beginners without proper instruction, so hire a professional if needed.

You will have to account for the countertop's finished height when cutting the front (vertical face) of the unit for the grill, as this will determine how deep you cut into the face of the unit. For this project, we used a 1¼-inch flagstone plus ½ inch of grout, so we adjusted the measurement 1¾ inches up for this cut. You only get one shot at cutting this, so double-check your measurements and use a triangle or straightedge to make sure you have 90-degree corners.

**STEP 9:** **Place the grill:** Drop in your grill and other components to make sure they fit. You will have to remove it so you can finish the countertop and vertical surfaces.

**STEP 10:** **Finish the vertical surfaces:** The best feature of these units is that they come prescratched, so they are ready to be stuccoed, tiled or veneered with stone. Your selected finish can greatly affect the overall look as well as the overall cost. Stucco is the most affordable option while natural stone is one of the more expensive finishes. For this unit, I used an architectural stone veneer (artificial stones) for the vertical and a natural flagstone cap for the counter.

**STEP 11:** **Fit the countertop:** You can use a lot of materials for the cap of your counter, such as tile, 1- to 2-inch-thick concrete or stone pavers, 2–3-inch-thick poured concrete or flagstone slabs. For this project we used flagstone slabs to match the other elements in the yard.

First lay out the flagstone on the countertop. Overlap edges as needed to get tight joints. You should plan on having ½- to ¾-inch grout spaces between each of the stones if possible and be sure to hang the flagstone 2½ inches over the edges or as needed to cover the vertical stone or whatever finish material you're using on the vertical sides. Use a pencil to sketch out where the chipped, uneven or overlapping edges are.

**STEP 12:** **Cut a natural edge:** Because this yard calls for a rustic look, having imperfect but "fitted" edges is ideal. Use a grinder, a wet saw or a mason's hammer to cut or trim down the edges to fit. We used a grinder to split the thin edge down the middle and then a mason's hammer to chip off the edges, giving it organic but linear edges. This is not a beginner DIY step, as the grinder can be dangerous, so opt to use a wet saw and rough up the edges with a mason's hammer if you are new to this tool. Also, it is possible to use just the mason's hammer to avoid sharp blades.

**STEP 13:** **Refit the countertop and mix the mortar:** After you finish cutting your stones, refit them so that they are overhanging with fairly consistent grout spaces. Mix up some type S mortar and some thinset separately in 5-gallon buckets.

**STEP 14:** **Build the base of the counter:** Because we are using a fairly thin natural stone, there are a lot of variations in thickness. Building up the base with mortar raises the stone but also gives us some play to adjust the level (if we just used thinset, we wouldn't have as much of a "cushion" to play with). Remove one or two stones at a time and use a trowel to place a thin layer of thinset on the surface of the counter, followed by a ½-inch layer of mortar.

**STEP 15:** **Apply the thinset:** Apply thinset to the back of the stone. The thinset offers superior adhesion to the stone and concrete—in essence, we are making a mortar sandwich.

**STEP 16:** **Place the stone:** Carefully place the stone back onto the mortar bed, matching up the grout joint spacing.

**STEP 17:** **Level the countertop:** Use a rubber mallet or the cushioned handle of a hand tool to tap the stone level to the desired height. Use a torpedo level to level the stones to each other.

**STEP 18:** **Connect and assemble the appliances:** Have a plumber and an electrician hook up all gas lines, electrical outlets and so forth. Place all your appliances and assemble per the manufacturers' instructions. Call your friends and have a barbecue at your new counter!

# SWINGING BAR SHELF WALL

### LEVEL: BEGINNER TO INTERMEDIATE
### COST: $$
### TIME COMMITMENT: WEEKEND
### PROFESSIONALS NEEDED: NONE
### DIMENSIONS: 6' LONG × 12" WIDE AT ITS WIDEST

This project is a lot of fun as it can be tailored to any area. If you have a small space, then you'll love the swinging bar shelf idea. I like installing outdoor shelves because they make the outdoor living space feel homey and decorated. This wall in particular was made out of Western red cedar, reclaimed wood from an old planter and wood from my fellow contractor's scrap pile. Any exterior-grade lumber can be substituted and fit together to make a rustic-style bar shelf. If you prefer a more modern look, stick with the same type of lumber and consistent finishes.

## TOOLS

- Safety glasses
- Tape measure
- Pencil
- Shovel
- 5-gallon buckets
- Level
- Miter saw or circular saw
- String line
- Brush for applying stain/sealer
- Drill
- Impact driver (optional)
- Speed square
- Metal drill bit (optional)
- Triangle
- Table saw
- Jigsaw (optional)
- Pocket hole jig (or use a countersink bit at an angle)

## MATERIALS

### CABINET STAND

- Six to eight 60-lb bags of concrete (for posts)
- Three 4" × 4" × 8' pressure-treated posts
- Three 4" × 4" metal post brackets (optional; I used pressure-treated lumber)
- Wood stain or sealer
- Two 2" × 6" × 12' cedar boards (double-check the spacing between posts before cutting), cut to the dimensions below:
  - Two cuts at 5'
  - Two cuts at 6'
- One 1-lb box of 3" exterior screws
- Two or four corbels (one on each side is functional, two on each side adds a decorative flair)

### SWINGING BAR SHELF

- One 1" × 12" × 10' piece of lumber, cut to 52"
- One 2" × 6" × 10' piece of lumber, cut to the dimensions below:
  - One cut to 45" (horizontal support)
  - One cut to 32" (vertical support)
  - One cut to 43" point to point with matching mitered edges (diagonal support)
- Two corbels (purchased or made from 2" × 6" lumber)
- Two exterior-grade brass 4" door hinges
- Two 4" × 4" × 10' pressure-treated posts
- Eight 80-lb bags of concrete (for posts)

### CABINET

- Four 2" × 7" tongue-and-groove scraps cut to 23½" (2" × 8" can be substituted)
- Wood glue
- Four metal stakes (optional, wood can be substituted)
- One 1-lb box of 1" exterior screws
- Two 2" × 12" scrap pieces cut to 23½" (any 2" × 12" material will do)
- Four exterior-grade powder-coated steel cabinet door hinges
- One 2" × 6" × 10' cedar boards cut to the dimensions below, or to fit your custom space:
  - Two cuts to 30" pieces (for top and bottom, wait to cut to verify your measurements until your cabinet is secure [step 10])
  - Two cuts to two 15" pieces (outer shelf [step 12])
- Two 1" × 8" × 6' new or reclaimed cedar fence boards (for back of shelf and actual interior shelves), cut to fit back and shelving to your liking

## CABINET STAND

**STEP 1:** **Select an area:** You'll want to place your bar near a gathering spot or in an area that is easy to access. Above an outdoor kitchen or attached between the posts of an overhead structure are great options as well. Both small and large spaces can be accommodated. Take measurements to adjust the cuts to your space, or follow the dimensions in this project if starting from scratch.

**STEP 2:** **Set the posts and seal the wood:** Dig two holes 24 inches deep and 12 to 14 inches wide, and mix up enough concrete, about four bags for each post, so that the concrete is at grade or slightly higher. Set the posts spaced 5 feet inside to inside, with at least 18 inches embedded in the concrete. If you live in an area that freezes, check your local code for recommendations on digging depths for posts.

Use a level to make sure they are plumb. You can set the pressure-treated post directly in concrete or use 4×4-inch brackets, which I recommend if you are not using pressure-treated lumber. Use a string line to match posts on the same plane and level. You can stain or seal all your lumber pieces while you wait for the post to set.

**STEP 3:** **Make the cuts and connect the posts:** Cut your lumber with a miter saw to the material list specifications but reference your installation, as your measurements are likely to have some variations. After the posts are set, using a drill and exterior screws, secure one 5-foot 2 × 6 so the top is level at 36 inches from the ground, and then secure the second 5-foot 2 × 6 at 23½ inches above the first. Verify the 90-degree angle with a speed square. Your cabinet will fit in this space.

## SWINGING BAR SHELF

STEP 4: **Install the swinging bar shelf:** This is very cool for how super simple it is. I used a piece of scrap 1 × 12-inch lumber cut to 52 inches. You can use any 1- to 2-inch-thick board. Attach the 45-inch 2 × 6 horizontal support to the underside of your bar shelf piece and then attach the 32-inch vertical support and 43-inch diagonal support. Create a corbel or two by cutting a 2 × 6 with a mitered edge. One is sufficient, but two makes it look more decorative. Attach two door hinges so that the turning peg sits proud (protruding just beyond the edge) of the 2 × 6.

STEP 5: **Attach the bar shelf to the stand:** Use an impact driver or drill to attach the two 4-inch hinges to the stand. Verify the angle with a speed square.

## CABINET

STEP 6: **Make the cabinet doors:** Mark the center of the bottom horizontal support spanning between the posts; this is where your cabinet doors will open. I used 2 × 7-inch tongue-and-groove cedar scraps, because this is an odd measurement; you'll probably be using 2 × 8-inch boards, which are actually 7½ inches wide, so your cabinet will measure 1 inch wider than this one. Use wood glue to attach two of your 23½-inch pieces.

**STEP 7:** **Attach the stakes to the cabinet doors:** The stakes reinforce the tongue-and-groove attachment, and are mostly decorative here, but necessary if using non-tongue-and-groove boards. These are just standard iron stakes that you can pick up at a landscape supply store. If they don't have holes, you can drill your own with a metal drill bit. Use 1-inch exterior screws and attach them starting at 3½ inches from the top/bottom, using a triangle to make sure they are plumb. Space the stakes about ⅛ inch away from the side, as the cabinet hinge will line up there. Assemble the other door the same way.

**STEP 8:** **Attach the cabinet sides:** Slide the two pieces of scrap 23½-inch lumber (or any new 2 × 12 × 23½-inch boards) in between the 2 × 6's horizontal supports. Use 3-inch exterior screws to secure from the top and bottom horizontal supports.

**STEP 9:** **Hang the doors:** Attach one cabinet door using the cabinet hinges lined up with the stakes, and adjust the spacing of the unit so that the door lines up just off-center of the mid mark by 1/16 inch or so. You need this space so that the doors clear each other when opened. Predrill holes and secure one side, and then repeat this step for the other side.

**STEP 10:** **Install the cabinet top and bottom:** Add a 2 × 6 to the top and bottom of the extruding part of the cabinet because your 23½-inch 2 × 12s extend beyond the back about 6 inches. Cut this to size lengthwise with the miter saw based on your dimensions; mine are roughly 30 inches. And don't forget to wear your safety glasses, unlike my buddy Denver here . . . come on, Denver, safety first!

**STEP 11:** **Install the cabinet back:** Using an old or new cedar fence board, measure and cut to fit the back of the cabinet. We have to split one board to 3¼ inches to fill the remaining gap. Use a jigsaw or table saw to "rip," or split, the fence board.

**STEP 12:** **Install the shelving:** Use the second fence board to create shelving for the inside. I plan on stocking whiskey for parties, so I made the unit scalable to a whiskey bottle and glasses. Get creative with this part, and figure out what you'd like to fit in your cabinet and whether you plan on keeping it permanently stocked or just set it up occasionally for entertaining. This is not a critter-resistant cabinet, and it can get hot in direct sun, so keep these aspects in mind. My cabinet is in a shaded part of the yard in a temperate climate. I don't plan on permanently storing booze here, but it's nice to have on hand.

I placed two additional shelves on either side of the cabinet for stability, but let me be honest: I just wanted more space for decorating. Slide the 15-inch 2 × 6 cedar boards into the middle and secure on the bottom using a pocket hole jig or a countersink bit at an angle to predrill the holes, and then secure with 3-inch screws.

Your swinging shelf is open for business. Break out the good stuff and toast your hard work!

# CHAPTER 2

# FIRE FEATURES
## KEEPING THE FLAME ALIVE

There is something about fire that brings people together. Whether the fire is offering warmth on a cold night or open flames for roasting marshmallows, it's sure to be encircled by family and friends. Simply watching the flames is mesmerizing and calming, which is why fire elements make such a great feature for any yard. Bringing fire to a yard can be as simple as adding fire accents like tiki torches or as bold as building a fireplace. There are plenty of options in between as well, such as freestanding metal fire pits and chimneys, which are easy to place in a landscape. Customizable gas-burning projects can be made with fire pans that can be incorporated into features such as tables, walls and pillars. Small accents such as candles and gel cans add charm and ambience. Your budget, available space and personal style should determine what makes the most sense for your home. This chapter will highlight some of the options for fire. I'll show you how to build a big impact fireplace (page 34) with minimal assembly skills and make your own fire pit using natural stones (page 40).

## OPTIONS FOR BRINGING FIRE TO THE YARD

**Fireplace.** Fireplaces can be one of the biggest investments when it comes to fire features, as they are large and labor-intensive, but they also have a big impact on the space. A fireplace provides not only a fire feature but also a focal point for an outdoor room. Fireplaces can be built from CMU block, brick or kits and can be fueled by wood, gas or propane. Gas is the most popular option because you don't have to clean up ashes and soot, as you would with a wood-burning fireplace, and most people investing in a fireplace don't want to hassle with refilling a propane tank. Usually, fireplaces are professionally installed by skilled masons; however, kits and prefabricated units are available to simplify the process, but they still take well-thought-out effort. Be picky when it comes to prefabricated units because they can look out of place if they don't match or fit your space well.

**Fire pit.** A fire pit is a universally appreciated feature that can easily meet many style preferences and budgets. Simple wood-burning fire pits can be made with materials like natural boulders (see page 76). A permanent feature is usually the most labor-intensive, but it can add the most value to a yard if it is done well. There are many prefabricated options, from affordable metal containers to heavy, permanent-looking features that can cost as much as or more than a custom-made pit.

**Fire feature.** Fire can be incorporated into a yard in a number of other ways as well, such as fire/water features, tiki torches or DIY decorative fire bowls made with gel cans.

## FUEL SOURCES AND MAINTENANCE

The three most popular fuel sources are natural gas, propane and wood. Gel cans are also available; these are smaller, decorative features that are easily replaced when spent. Since most fire features are made out of stone, metal or concrete, you don't need to worry too much about maintaining the finish. Applying sealer on natural stone every few years can help prevent staining from grease or other oily products.

**Natural gas.** This is the premium choice for fire features because it is clean and simple to use. Once you pull the gas line and hook it up, the maintenance is fairly nonexistent. Natural gas is a bit pricier because you have to trench for gas lines and pull permits, but you'll never need to fill up another propane tank or clean up a sooty wood fire again.

**Propane.** Propane is a good choice for many homeowners because it is easy to use and easy to clean up, plus it drops the price point. All you need to do is hook up a propane tank to the fire source. Make sure you plan for an area to hide the tank, or build it into the design. Propane requires regular filling. A 20# propane tank will last around four hours when set at maximum output and about double that time if set at medium output.

**Wood.** This classic choice always remains in style. The smell of burning wood and the taste of wood-fire-roasted marshmallows light up the senses. However, there is the cleanup, smell and soot to deal with each time it is used.

**TIP:** *Roasting marshmallows or grilling hot dogs over gas fire pits is not recommended because the rocks or glass in a fire pit are permanent features, and grease or goo can clog the pores of the fire ring.*

# FIREPLACE KIT

**LEVEL: INTERMEDIATE TO ADVANCED**
**COST: $$$$**
**TIME COMMITMENT: 2-4 WEEKENDS**
**PROFESSIONALS NEEDED: PLUMBER (FOR GAS LINE, IF USING), ELECTRICIAN (IF RUNNING ELECTRICAL)**
**DIMENSIONS: 37" DEEP × 68" LONG × 81" HIGH**

Building a fireplace from a kit simplifies the process. Your time is well spent for the payoff of having your very own fireplace at a lower price. There are a few different kits and prefabricated units on the market, and this in particular is one of my favorites because the assembly is straightforward and it's customizable. With some helping hands, it will take only an hour or two to assemble the base unit. This is a sturdy system, so enlist a couple of strong friends to help you out (trade them beer for labor—it always works for me!).

The exterior of the fireplace kit is prescratched and ready to take a variety of finishes, so you can customize it to your personal style and the ambience of your yard. Because a fireplace is such a significant feature, it is important to consider the rest of your yard and the architecture of your house. Stucco, tile, stone, stone veneer or a combination are all good finish options. For this project, I used an architectural stone veneer that is lightweight and rustic in combination with a natural stone cap and details.

The mantel is an important focal point on any fireplace. For the mantel in this project, I didn't want to introduce another finish material, which could be distracting to the overall look, but I wanted to add interest and detail. So, using scrap pieces of stone from chiseling and cutting the flagstone cap, I created a mantel mosaic—the steps are included here for you to get the same attractive effect.

## TOOLS

- Tape measure
- 2'-3' level
- Crescent wrench and socket set
- 5-gallon buckets
- Drill with mixing paddle
- Square or triangle trowel
- Torpedo level (mini level)
- Mason's hammer or grinder with diamond blade
- Rubber gloves
- 5-gallon bucket
- Zip-top sandwich bag
- Wooden ledge (optional)
- Grouting bag
- Sponge

## MATERIALS

### FIREPLACE

- Fireplace kit (37" deep × 68" long × 81" high)
- Fireplace extensions, such as extended benches, seat backs, extended hearth, chimney extension (optional)
- Plastic shims
- ¾" nuts and bolts (available with kit)
- Stone veneer mortar (type S with admixtures)
- Stone finish of choice
- Stone caps of choice
- Decorative accents of choice (optional)

### MANTEL MOSAIC

- Stone scraps
- One 50-lb bag of thinset
- One 25-lb bag of colored sanded grout

## FIREPLACE

STEP 1: **Select your location and fireplace unit:** Most cities and towns have restrictions on where you can place a fire structure on your property, so check your local municipality for setbacks (how far the fireplace needs to be from other structures) and permits. Measure your space and select your kit and kit extensions or extras. This unit has additional bench backs and a chimney extension to make it a more significant piece of the yard. Don't be intimidated by the size: a fireplace should be large. If your space has a solid surface like a concrete floor, you're all set. If not, pour a concrete footing at least 4 inches deep and 2 inches wider than the unit on each side. Again, if the ground in your area freezes, check the code for requirements. If you are installing a gas fireplace, bring in a licensed plumber to pull the gas line and connect the unit. This usually requires a permit.

STEP 2: **Assemble the kit:** Assemble the fireplace unit following the manufacturer's directions. This kit is very similar in assembly to the grill counter (see page 20). Start by measuring and placing the bottom level of boxes. Make sure they are square, plumb and in line or parallel with your space, because you will not be able to move them once you stack the top units. You will need two to four people to move these pieces into place and stack them. Use plastic shims and a level to adjust as needed for a level surface. With a crescent wrench, secure the units with the bolts provided in the kit.

STEP 3: **Select the finish:** Because the units are prescratched you can install the finish immediately. For this fireplace I used a combination of natural stone for the caps and artificial (aka architectural) stone for the verticals. Sometimes matching real stone with artificial stone can highlight their differences, and not in a good way, so look at your samples in different lighting to make sure they're a good match. This project uses Pennsylvania lilac flagstone, Buffstone Minaret architectural stone veneer and a coffee-colored mortar because I am not filling the joints with grout.

### FINISH OPTIONS

Stucco is the most affordable option for finishing an outdoor project, and a small upgrade to a smooth Santa Barbara stucco finish can make it look like concrete for a modern flair. Classic tiles or even a mosaic are fun options, too. Natural stone, stacked or placed flat, is a safe choice because it is an appealing and timeless material.

**STEP 4: Mix the mortar:** The best way to attach natural or artificial stone is with a type S mortar with color and polymer additives to make it extra sticky and to look attractive if it peeks through the joints. The added color is great if you don't plan on grouting. Tan and brown are the most available options, but pick something that will match or complement your chosen finish. Mix the mortar with water in a 5-gallon bucket using a drill with a mixing paddle. You want a thick peanut butter–like consistency that will stick to the trowel when you flick the tool with your wrist.

**STEP 5: Adhere the veneer:** Because the surface is already scratched, apply the mortar to the back of the stone, using a trowel to make a slight peak 1 to 1½ inches tall; this will be compressed when the stone is pressed onto the surface. Start at the bottom corner of the fireplace with a corner piece and work your way across. Always set the corners first and then work inward. This allows you to hide some cuts in the middle if the stones don't fit perfectly. The bottom layer will help hold up the top layers so they don't sag down the wall as you work; you can use chips of stone or wood as temporary shims if needed for leveling. You get only one chance to put up the veneer, unless you make some adjustments while it is still wet, so once it is set, you won't be able to remove it cleanly.

**STEP 6: Check your level:** Your mini and long levels should be your guides when you are working close up, but when placing individual stones, it is important to check your overall level by stepping back to look every few rows and making sure you're not placing them at an angle. A slanted row is a true rookie move and is not easily remedied.

**TIP:** *If you're not sure if your mortar is still workable, test to see if it is tacky by pressing your finger lightly into the mix. Some mortar should stick to your finger. If none sticks to your finger and you just leave an indentation, then the mortar is no longer at full adhesive strength. It's time to mix up some new mortar. Avoid rewetting or mixing the old with the new because this can affect the strength of the mix. And don't mix too much at a time, in order to reduce waste.*

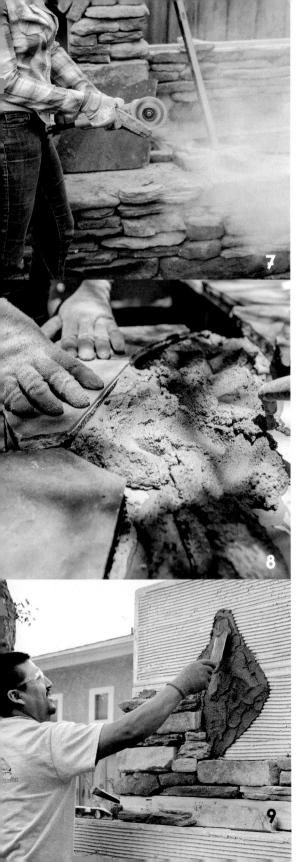

STEP 7: **Fit and cut the stones:** Not all of the stones are going to fit perfectly, so you may need to cut them to fit. A grinder is the most efficient and accurate machine for this task, but it is not a beginner's tool and can be fairly dangerous and is best left for the experienced or professionals. A mason's hammer and/or a chisel work great as an alternative; you'll just need a little patience to chip and shape your stones as needed. Try to hide the cut pieces as much as you can; if using an artificial stone veneer, the inside is not the same color or texture as the outside, so be strategic.

STEP 8: **Cap it off:** The bench/hearth and all other horizontal areas should be finished with a cap. Poured concrete, prefabricated concrete slabs/caps and flagstone are all great choices. If you want a poured concrete cap, do this before adhering the vertical finish so you have room to build the removable lumber forms. This project uses 1½-inch thick flagstone pieces cut and fit together with a consistent grout line. Wait at least a day or more before grouting.

STEP 9: **Add accents:** The mantel and the face of the chimney are great areas to add accents. It's nice to break up these spaces with alternating or different materials to make the piece more dynamic and visually interesting. We used the same flagstone that we used for the horizontal surfaces/caps and placed it in the center of the chimney face. Since this project has a rustic look, we left the edges natural and rough.

## MOSAIC MANTEL

**STEP 1:** **Sort the mosaic scraps:** Start by sorting your pieces of scrap into piles based on size. Let your cut pieces inspire your layout. I hardly altered any of these pieces and simply based my design on what was available.

**STEP 2:** **Mix the thinset:** Put on rubber gloves. In a 5-gallon bucket, mix up a thick batch of thinset according to the manufacturer's instructions, let sit for 10 minutes and then remix. I let my thinset get really sticky so that it can hold the weight of the stone pieces. Try not to get too messy, though, because the thinset will dry white and look sloppy if it peeks through the grout. When working with small stones, I fill a sandwich bag with thinset and apply it in dabs to the back of the stone. Also, make sure your gloves match your shirt . . . just kidding!

**STEP 3:** **Place the stones:** Start in the center with a few key pieces, as this will be the focal point. After making progress on the center, place the edge pieces and move back in toward the middle, mirroring the size and shape of the stones on either side. If the stones are slipping, place a wooden ledge at the bottom to temporarily hold the pieces in place until they set up.

**STEP 4:** **Grout:** Let the stones set overnight before you grout. Use a colored sanded grout to blend with the overall fireplace. Mix the grout so that it moves smoothly into the joints. Using a grouting bag, squeeze out the grout and fill any voids. Use a damp sponge to press the grout into the joints, especially in difficult and detailed areas like the accent in the center. This will leave a concrete residue, so use a separate clean damp sponge to pick up the residue, rinsing and wringing after each wipe.

# NATURAL STONE FIRE PIT

**LEVEL: INTERMEDIATE TO ADVANCED**
**COST: $-$$**
**TIME COMMITMENT: 1-2 WEEKENDS**
**PROFESSIONALS NEEDED: PLUMBER (FOR GAS LINE, IF USING),
ELECTRICIAN (IF RUNNING ELECTRICAL)**
**DIMENSIONS: 4½' DIAMETER**

A natural stone fire pit is a nice balance of rustic and modern. It is a permanent structure that will withstand a lot of long-term use. For this fire pit I ran a gas line, but you could make a wood-burning pit by omitting the gas line and the fire ring insert. I used natural stones that I found on the property, which was great because we didn't need to buy them and their appearance ties the fire pit into the natural landscape.

BEFORE

## TOOLS

- Masonry string or other flexible rope/string
- Metal stake
- Shovel
- 5-gallon buckets
- Level
- Drill with mixing paddle
- Hand trowel
- Brick saw or angle grinder
- Grout bag
- Sponge

## MATERIALS

- One can of marking spray
- Ten 80-lb bags of concrete
- 1½ cubic yards of 4–6" natural round stones
- Three 94-lb bags of type S mortar
- 60–70 firebricks
- Four 50-lb bags of ¾" gravel
- 1¼ cubic yards of large 4–8" lava rock or other filler, such as broken bricks and concrete scraps
- 36" fire ring
- ½ cubic yard of small ½–2" lava rock
- About seventeen 2"-thick 12" × 12" flagstones (to be cut to fit)
- 75 lb of fire glass, any color
- 3½" fire key if running gas

**STEP 1: Select your location:** Consider making your fire pit the focal point of your yard. I like to use it to anchor the center of a space or place it in an area that is inviting and visible from the house. If you plan on using natural gas, have a plumber run the piping to the location so that the stem or output will be placed within the walls of your fire ring. Place it roughly where you'd like to keep the key that turns it on.

**STEP 2: Create the footing:** Mark a 3½-foot inside ring and a 4½-foot outside ring by attaching a string to a metal stake secured in the middle of the pit. Use marking spray as you walk around in a circle. (If the ground is very dry, mist it with a hose first for better adhesion.) If you're running a gas line, have your plumber run it in between your marked lines so it's built into the structure. After the circle is marked out, dig out an area 6 inches deep and 1 foot wide. Dig down deeper to match local frost-line requirements in areas that freeze. Mix up concrete bags in a 5-gallon bucket and fill the circular trench with concrete. Smooth and level the top and leave to harden.

**STEP 3: Create the first layer:** Set the first ring of 4- to 6-inch natural stones to sit on the outside edge of the concrete footing. The stones can overlap to the outside, if needed. Mix up a medium-size batch of mortar in a 5-gallon bucket using a drill with a mixing paddle. Adhere the firebrick horizontally to the concrete footing with the mortar, spreading it on with a trowel. Use the mortar and a torpedo level to level each brick to the next until you have a complete circle. You will have to use a brick saw to cut a few bricks so that you can complete the circle. All the bricks should be touching on the inside of the circle, so the outside will have open gaps, which should be filled with mortar. Sponge off excess mortar protruding from the top of the bricks. Next, add a 2- to 4-inch layer of ¾-inch gravel as filler and drainage.

**STEP 4:** **Make the second layer:** Loosely fit firebricks vertically around the ring so you can adjust them as needed. Set the firebricks with the mortar, leveling as you go. You will have big gaps in the back and the front will mostly be touching. If you want a shorter fire pit or are making a wood-burning fire pit, stop here and remember that your cap will add 2 to 3 inches to the final height. Ideally, your fire pit should be 2 to 4 inches below the benches or chairs that surround it so that you can lean toward it or prop your feet up on the ring. Since I plan on raising the ground around this one, I added another layer of stacked bricks cut to 6 inches and staggered the seams when setting the mortar on top of the previous layer. Check the level as you work. This is important.

**STEP 5:** **Add the natural stone:** After the first, second and some of the third layer of firebricks are set up, mortar the natural stone along the exterior wall. Start on the bottom and work your way around. Put a nice 1- to 2-inch-thick layer of mortar on the back of each stone and be sure to fill all the gaps between the bricks with mortar. You will have to fit the stones together like a puzzle. Take your time and enjoy the process.

**STEP 6:** **Fill the pit:** Fill the bottom of the pit with any scrap bricks and about nine bags of large 4- to 8-inch lava rocks. You can also use broken concrete, scrap bricks or other fillers if you place them on the lower portion. I like to keep the lava rock near the ring because it is best suited for the heat . . . I mean, it came from a volcano, a little fire won't hurt it!

**STEP 7:** **Attach the ring and test:** Have your licensed plumber connect your gas lines and attach your fire ring.

**STEP 8:** **Fill with smaller gravel:** Now that the fire ring is installed, continue by filling in the voids between the bigger lava rocks with about a 2-inch layer of small lava rocks. You want these voids filled so you don't lose your precious—and expensive—collection of fire glass to the bottom of the pit where no one can appreciate it. Level everything off to about the height of your fire ring.

**STEP 9:** **Add the flagstone cap:** Select a flagstone piece that is roughly 2 inches thick by roughly 12 inches wide and 12 inches across. Lay out all the pieces on top of the fire pit. Mark where they overlap and cut with a brick saw, allowing a ½-inch gap between them for grout. Adhere the flagstone to the top with thinset and let it set for 24 hours before returning to grout. We used type S mortar for the grout and applied it between the joints with a grout bag and cleaned up any overflow with a damp sponge as we worked.

**STEP 10:** **Decorate with colored glass:** Add a pop of color with a 1- to 2-inch layer of fire glass. I used four different colors of reflective glass to create a fun design that covers the fire ring insert. Fire glass is expensive, around $50 per gallon, but nothing beats the finished look. Insert the fire key and turn it to enjoy your fire pit. Look forward to the future memories that will be made here, sitting under the stars and toasting your toes!

## MAKE A PROPANE- OR WOOD-BURNING FIRE RING

This fire pit can be adapted for propane fuel or wood. Propane is the exact same setup, except that you don't need a plumber to pull a gas line. Instead, you attach the fire ring to a propane fuel source. Find an area or build a box to hide or contain your propane tank. For a wood-burning fire pit, you don't need fuel lines, fire rings, lava rocks or fire glass, but build the pit lower by 4 to 6 inches so that you get more access to the flames.

# CHAPTER 3

# WATER FEATURES
## THE SOUND AND SOURCE OF LIFE

Both the sound and the beauty of water have a relaxing and cooling effect on a space. We are so reliant on water that we can't help but be drawn to it. The sound of water trickling down the face of a rock will soothe your senses and draw wildlife to your home.

Although everyone likes the idea of a water feature in their yard, not everyone is prepared for the maintenance and responsibility it requires. Things to consider when adding a water feature to your home are safety for children, maintenance and overall upkeep. Some features require comparatively little maintenance, such as a self-contained ceramic fountain, while others require regular attention, such as a koi pond or water wall, which can be time-consuming and expensive. This chapter will explore them all. If you are looking at water features as something that will add value to your home, remember that the amount of responsibility and maintenance required for larger projects can be a turnoff to potential buyers . . . or they might absolutely love the feature. Small features don't really make a monetary impact but can certainly add to the ambience and create a wholesome and relaxing environment that is priceless, and the project for a Disappearing Water Basin Fountain (page 46) will help you achieve it.

## WATER FEATURE OPTIONS

Water features can take so many forms, from natural stone waterfalls to a self-contained unit to a koi pond. Choosing what is right for you and your yard will come down to preference. Here are just a few popular options.

**Pond.** You can create a small pond by buying a prefabricated plastic basin or by placing a pond liner over a trenched hole; then you simply fill it with water and add a pump. More complex or larger ponds with plants and animal life are really amazing and create an interactive environment that will transform your yard.

**Fountain.** Prefabricated features come in so many different styles—from traditional tiered systems to modern angular forms—that there is something for every yard. Fountains are relatively easy to assemble, add a beautiful focal point and fill the space with the relaxing sound of water. Disappearing water basin fountains are also popular, as it appears that water is flowing out of a container and into the ground (see page 46). Or you can choose almost any open container you like and customize it to your yard.

**Water wall.** These are a favorite of mine! They are typically built with CMU blocks on a concrete footing and feature a concrete basin with a stone veneer. Water trickles its way down the front, collects in the basin and recirculates. Water walls can be small focal pieces or large spreads that can provide a "wall" for an outdoor room. These are a lot of work compared to a prefabricated fountain but are impactful and stunning.

## MAINTENANCE CONSIDERATIONS

Depending on your system, all water features require some maintenance, and some require a lot more than others. Lower maintenance options include prefabricated fountains and water walls, which require periodic cleaning. My go-to expert on water features, Carl Petite of Colombia Water Gardens, recommends using a power washer to clean off any buildup and letting the feature dry out. There are also water treatment options that can help reduce the growth of algae and other undesirables.

Ponds and waterfalls need more attention, especially if you have plants or animals living in them. You can upset the ecological balance with too many chemicals but you also need to keep the algae down and ward off mosquito populations. Seek out your local pond supply store for recommendations depending on the plant and animal life in your pond, as recommendations will vary. Expect about the same amount of maintenance as a pool, that is, skimming the surface for debris, brushing the sides to inhibit algae buildup, vacuuming the bottom to remove slime, changing filters, checking water levels and pH balance and more.

Your local environment will greatly affect the maintenance requirements of your water feature. For example, hot or sunny climates will have a faster evaporation rate, shady or woody areas will have heavy leaf litter and freezing temperatures will require winterization and the replanting of annual plants. All of these tasks and more need to be taken into consideration when planning your feature.

## PUMPS

All water features need movement or they will become stagnant mosquito ponds. An electric pump is the most popular way to make this happen, but your favorite area may not have electricity. There are solar options for powering your pump if it is in a sunny environment. Pumps not only create water movement to keep mosquitos away, but they also allow you to adjust the overall effect of the water feature, from quietly burbling water to a gushing fountain, by selecting the setting, the strength of the pump and how many gallons of water you keep moving.

Here are some examples:

- A 2-foot-wide by 4-foot-tall recirculating fountain feature in a basin uses a 1,000-gallon-per-hour (GPH) pump with an adjustable flow control so you can adjust whether it calmly rolls over the edge or shoots up and flows over.

- A 4-foot-wide by 7-foot-tall recirculating water wall uses an 8,400-GPH pump that sits behind the wall in a concrete basin.

- A waterfall feature requires a pump that can move 100 gallons of water per hour per horizontal inch of waterfall. So, if the fall is 36 inches wide, you need a 3,600-GPH pump. When in doubt, estimate up, because you can adjust your water feature down but can't turn up the GPH.

- A 10 × 10 × 2-foot pond is about 1,100 gallons in total, and you need all the water to recirculate four or five times within an hour, so you'll need a 4,000- to 5,000-GPH pump. Larger ponds do not necessarily require such a large turnover rate, so a pond twice this size would still be adequately recirculated at this flow rate. In any case, you'll need to contact a professional in your area for recommendations.

# DISAPPEARING WATER BASIN FOUNTAIN

**LEVEL: BEGINNER**
**COST: $$**
**TIME COMMITMENT: 1 DAY**
**PROFESSIONALS NEEDED: ELECTRICIAN**
**(TO PLACE AN EXTERIOR OUTLET, IF NEEDED)**
**DIMENSIONS: 3' × 4'**

A disappearing fountain system is a great project for any yard because it's relatively low maintenance and fairly straightforward to assemble—the hardest part is digging the hole! Since the top feature is interchangeable, you can choose from a plethora of design styles and sizes. In no time, you'll have a pleasant-sounding water feature that will make you think you're sitting beside a burbling brook in the privacy of your own yard. For a taller feature than the one shown here, or if you want a bubbling effect, use PVC pipe instead of vinyl tubing.

BEFORE

## TOOLS

- Gloves
- Shovel
- Tape measure
- Hand tamper
- Rake or scrap 2" × 4" to level
- 2' level

## MATERIALS

- Plastic basin with perforated cover (you can buy these in the garden department of a local store or online)
- Glazed ceramic pot, ideally 2' to 5' tall
- Decorative feature to sit on top of basin (drilled with hole, if necessary)
- Ten 50-lb bags of base material
- Three 50-lb bags of masonry sand
- 1,000- to 1,200-GPH pump with adjustable flow control
- 6' PVC pipe or vinyl tube (should be 1'-2' longer than the height of your fountain piece)
- One 10-oz tube of silicone caulking
- Ten 30-lb bags of 2"-3" decorative stones
- Fittings appropriate to your style of fountain

**STEP 1:** **Select your location:** Locate your fountain near a ground fault circuit interrupter (GFCI) outlet or hire an electrician to place an exterior outlet for your feature to plug into. Consider placing your fountain in your front yard or near the door as a welcoming feature, and it will remind you to leave your work stressors outside the home. Another great location is outside the master bedroom window or near gathering areas to get the maximum benefit.

**STEP 2:** **Select your decorative feature:** Your decorative feature sits on top of the basin, and it is the only piece of the feature you will see because the basin will be buried. This can be any ceramic pot, natural stone piece or other water-appropriate container. It can be tall or short, wide mouth or narrow mouth and of course any color or shape. Natural stone features such as basalt or a boulder will need to have a hole drilled all the way through the piece. Based on the size and weight of your feature, you will need to select a basin so it can accommodate the weight. Your selected decorative piece should always sit well within your basin so that splashing water is collected. For this project I used a 4-foot-tall ceramic pot, as it adds a pop of color and is easy to set in place.

**STEP 3:** **Excavate the hole:** Dig a hole about 3 inches wider and deeper than your basin. If you live in an area with heavy clay soil or ground that freezes, widen your hole to at least 6 inches all around to help absorb the swelling and contracting of the soil. Backfill the hole with 2 inches of base material and compact it with a hand tamper. Add 1 inch of masonry sand. Use a piece of lumber or a rake to loosely level the sand and compact it with the hand tamper.

**STEP 4:** **Place, level and backfill the basin:** Drop your basin into the hole and check your level. Use additional handfuls or shovelfuls of sand to correct your grade as needed. Make sure your basin is as level as possible; this is important for the stability of the decorative feature that sits on top, as well as to have sheering of water flow. Use a shovel to backfill the sides of the basin with soil; if you have a heavy clay soil or get freezing temperatures, use gravel instead. If your feature is very heavy, consider placing a CMU block in the basin under where it will sit.

**STEP 5:** **Seal the basin and install the decorative feature:** Run the vinyl tube from the bottom of the container to about 2 inches past the top of the water feature. Seal the connection between the hole in the bottom of the pot and the vinyl tube with silicone. Let the silicone cure overnight, or as specified by the manufacturer. Place the perforated lid on the basin and position the decorative feature upright. Line up your vinyl tube with the hole in the top of the basin, making sure not to pinch it under the pot. If you are using a ceramic decorative piece, fill the inside with stones to weight it down and stabilize it. Don't bend and pinch the vinyl tube as you fill the decorative feature with stones, and fill it up only one-half to three-fourths of the way. Check your level and use shims to even it out if necessary.

**STEP 6:** **Set up the pump:** Place the pump and select the appropriate fitting for your vinyl tube; I used a ½-inch tube and fitting for this fountain. You can also use a PVC pipe and fittings if you'd like the water to bubble up at the top rather than just roll over, like this one does. Attach your pump to the vinyl tube with a little bit of pressure. Then place your pump on the bottom of the container so it can recirculate the water.

**STEP 7:** **Add rocks:** Add the decorative stones on the top of the basin cover: this is what makes the water look as if it's disappearing! The decorative stones should be big enough so that they don't fall through the perforations on the basin cap and should spread beyond the basin to hide the plastic underneath. Add more stones to the inside of the container to position the vinyl tube in a relatively upright position, or if using PVC, cut 1 to 2 inches below the lip of the decorative feature for a seamless, bubbling-over effect.

**STEP 8:** **Add water and test:** Fill up your basin with water and turn on your pump. You're testing to make sure your connections are good and there aren't any leaks. Adjust the flow of water to your preference. Pull up a chair and enjoy!

# CHAPTER 4

# OVERHEAD STRUCTURES

## ABOVE AND BEYOND

Traditionally built out of wood, overhead structures create scale in an open space. They focus energy and draw attention to a certain area as they pull you in and welcome you to stay. There is something very comforting about having a structure surround you, even if it's open. Of course, there are plenty of functional benefits, too, with covered canopies providing protection from the elements.

Adding an overhead structure is like adding square footage to a home by way of an exterior room. Of course, you will not be able to appraise the addition as you would with an extra bedroom, but it does have its benefits. Homes with well-maintained outdoor structures have perceived value and an undeniable ambience. If the structure is well built and maintained, it will become a permanent feature of your residence. This chapter will explore the various forms an outdoor structure can take, such as a pergola, an arbor or a trellis; explore what you'll need to consider for your space; explain the various material options, including wood, metal, steel, aluminum, plastic and vinyl; and discuss the various add-on features available, such as lighting and décor options. I'll show you how to build a simple overhead structure (page 54), so you can start experiencing the benefits of a protected outdoor room right away.

# PERGOLAS VERSUS ARBORS VERSUS TRELLISES

The terms *pergola*, *arbor* and *trellis* are used interchangeably by homeowners and professionals alike, so to clear up the confusion, here is a list of the features that distinguish each of these.

**Pergola:** This is an overhead structure that can have an enclosed or semi-open roof. It can be attached to a house or freestanding. Usually the intent is for protection or filtration from the elements and to create outdoor rooms. This section of the book is focused mainly on pergolas, as they are the most impactful outdoor living features.

**Arbor:** This is usually a smaller structure that frames pathways, entrances or focal points. An arbor is usually combined with trellis sides so that vines and plants can be trained to grow over the top, but not always.

**Trellis:** This is an open latticework system that's intended for plants or vines to climb on. It does not have an overhead structure. Trellises are freestanding or can be part of a larger structure. For example, a pergola might have a vertical trellis wall built into it on one side for a vine to grow up, or an arbor might have a trellis on either side for vines to climb up and over the structure.

## ANATOMY OF AN OVERHEAD STRUCTURE

Since I'll be focusing on pergolas in this chapter, you'll need to know the names of the various structures that make up a pergola. Referring to the structures correctly means you'll be able to communicate well with your supplier or contractor. Here are the most commonly used terms for the composition of a basic pergola.

**Post:** Posts are the vertical supports of the structure and usually take the brunt of the weight of the system.

**Beams:** Beams are attached on either side of a post and provide the base for the crossbeams or rafters.

**Crossbeams or rafters:** These attach to the beams in the opposite direction, providing support and strength to the structure.

**Purlins or lattice:** These are decorative elements that reinforce the previous layer. They are optional but can add extra shade and detail to the structure.

**Ledger board:** A ledger board is used only when the structure is being attached to a home or building. The ledger helps disperse the weight of the structure and reduces the number of attachments that are needed, as the rafters tie into the ledger board.

**Corbels:** These are typically optional decorative pieces but can be structural if they attach to the post and beam.

**Gussets or elbows:** These are braces that strengthen the corners of the structure. Depending on how it's built, these may be necessary or optional.

**Boots:** These are optional decorative wraps that go around the base of the post to hide metal brackets or simply to add detail and interest.

## BUILDING CONSIDERATIONS

Structures can be built out of many different materials and in many different styles. They can have full covers, open covers or no covers at all. This all greatly affects the mood and feel of the yard, whether it feels open and airy or enclosed and sheltered. When thinking about adding a structure to your home, figure out what your space needs and what you and your family want. Do you need shade, or will a structure block too much sunlight? Should you attach it to the back of the house or have a freestanding space further away in the yard?

Most people prefer to have their outdoor room near the actual home to create a progression from a formal atmosphere (home) to a semi-informal environment (outdoor room) to natural and informal surroundings (yard). Also think about what activities you imagine happening in your space. Are you hoping to dine, lounge or cook in your structure? The opportunities are many!

Think about your style and the style of your home. Modern, traditional and rustic can all look very different and each can be achieved beautifully with the right inspiration and material choices. But it won't be appealing if the outdoor structure differs dramatically in style and materials from the house, so aim to have a more unified look.

## OPEN VERSUS COVERED

Probably the most important decision you'll make is whether the structure should be open or have a roof that encloses it. There are pros and cons to each option.

**Open.** This structure's beams have the rafters/crossbeams and sometimes purlins attached, making it open or semi-open. The covers offer an airier, lighter and filtered atmosphere that is a little less formal than a fully covered structure. The benefits are that you still get the feel and shape of an outdoor room but you also get light below and into any windows if attached to a house. A semi-open cover can usually be modified to a solid cover with plastic or metal panels attached above the rafters.

**Covered.** This structure offers a lot more protection from the natural elements, such as snow, rain and sun. It tends to cost quite a bit more, depending on the materials, but may be worth the extra investment if it allows you to use it more or for a longer season. Another benefit of a covered roof is reduced leaf litter and less exposure to the elements for the furniture and decor. Covers can vary from traditional shingled roofs to tongue-and-groove cedar or redwood to solid aluminum or vinyl panels. In areas with mild weather, stretching a canvas across the top of a simple semi-open structure and attaching it with staples can offer some protection while still keeping it light and airy.

## OPTIONS FOR BUILDING MATERIALS

The type of building material you choose will greatly affect the look and feel of your outdoor structure, so take some time and investigate all the options. Wood is often the most obvious choice, but beautiful outdoor structures can be built from various metals and plastics as well.

**Wood.** Lumber is the traditional choice. Most structures are built from cedar, redwood, mahogany, ipe or pressure-treated wood, which are all tough and reliable choices (see Chapter 7 for more on lumber). Douglas fir is another popular option because of price. It's structurally sound, but more susceptible to insects and rot, so maintenance and upkeep are key. The downside to all wood is its potential to rot or attract termites. You'll need to apply paint, stain or oil yearly or every few years depending on the wood type and the amount of exposure to the elements. However, a well-maintained wood structure can last a long time, and you can't beat the classic choice in terms of aesthetics.

**Metal.** In terms of strength and maintenance, metal is a great choice. However, it can get hot to the touch in direct sun; but then again, do you really need to touch your pergola? Steel and aluminum are two solid choices. (See Chapter 8 to learn more about metal.) Keep in mind these structures typically need engineering.

- **Steel.** Nothing screams modern more than a simple steel structure. A steel feature will have a big impact on the entire the yard, really driving the design aesthetic of your home. And it can have just as big an impact on your budget. Because these structures are typically custom-made, quite heavy, have high material costs and require a structural engineer to design or approve the plans, the costs add up quickly. The structure must be bolted or welded together and you should use galvanized or powder-coated steel to keep it from rusting. However, if you use corten steel, you might want to let it rust naturally to a nice orange and then seal it to keep that color or else it will rust to a soft dark brown.

- **Aluminum.** Aluminum structures are a popular option, and the cost is comparable to or slightly higher than that of lumber, but the low to no maintenance in the long run is a big selling point. They are usually lightweight and strong and come in many colors, plus they can be painted whatever color you like. These structures are usually part of a kit, so you are typically limited to the prefabricated design. Overall, it is a nice hire or DIY system that is affordable, semi-customizable and low maintenance.

**Plastic.** Plastic structures are popular because they are low maintenance, do not rot, do not rust and have no issues with insect damage. Plastic structures are long lasting, and because plastic doesn't swell and contract with moisture like wood does, there are fewer issues with paint chipping off. However, they do warp slightly with temperature fluctuations and have a different feel than standard lumber features.

- **Cellular PVC.** This material is similar to wood in the way that it can be manipulated and cut. It is typically white and paintable.

- **Vinyl.** Another synthetic option is vinyl. It is usually available as prefabricated and molded pieces that are assembled in a kit, so a vinyl structure is less customizable; however, this won't be an issue if you are sticking to standard dimensions.

## ADD-ON OPTIONS

This is the fun part. What would you like in your structure that will take it to the next level and make it a truly comfortable place to be? Here are some options.

**Lights.** Functionally, lights will allow you to use your outdoor space longer into the evening. Placing decorative lights such as bistro lights or up and down lights can also be useful and enhance the design. Inset or can lights really step it up, making it more contemporary and expensive.

**Ceiling fan.** A ceiling fan can be a great addition in areas with warm weather and it makes it harder for bugs to hang around and join the party. This is only recommended for covered structures.

**Misters.** Misters are a lot of fun for kids of all ages. They can really cool down a space on a hot day or evening. Assembly can be relatively easy, too.

**Space heaters.** These are a great option for cool evenings. They can be upright standing heaters, inset into the roof or hanging from the structure. Not all structural materials can handle the extra heat and weight, so check with the manufacture before purchasing.

# SIMPLE AND MODERN OVERHEAD STRUCTURE

**LEVEL: INTERMEDIATE TO ADVANCED**
**COST: $$$**
**TIME COMMITMENT: WEEKEND**
**PROFESSIONALS NEEDED: NONE**
**DIMENSIONS: 14' × 12'**

This modern pergola is simple and striking. It is not traditional, as most pergolas have layers in the overhead structure, for both aesthetics and stability. However, if you are building a smaller structure in an area that doesn't have the additional weight of snow or other debris that can weigh it down, you can really simplify the construction and use joist hangers instead of layering wood for a clean, streamlined style. Using bigger lumber posts (as opposed to 4 × 4s) gives it extra strength and a bold look. Lumber has the tendency to sag over long distances, so gussets help to mitigate this. I don't recommend spanning more than about 12 feet with 2 × 6s without upgrading to bigger, wider wood and/or adding gussets.

**BEFORE**

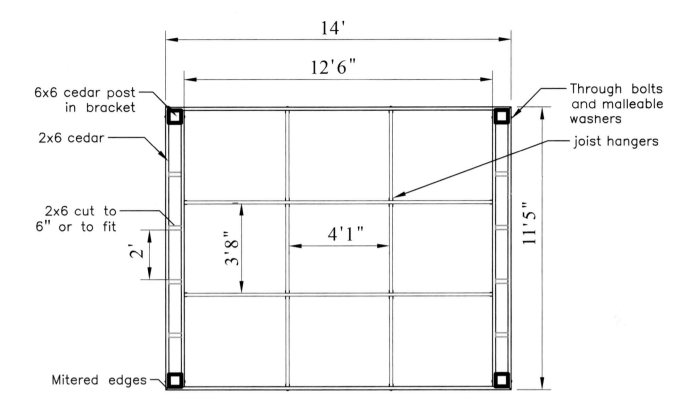

Diagram labels:

- 6x6 cedar post in bracket
- 2x6 cedar
- 2x6 cut to 6" or to fit
- Mitered edges
- Through bolts and malleable washers
- joist hangers

Dimensions: 14', 12'6", 11'5", 3'8", 4'1", 2'

## TOOLS

- Gloves
- Shovel
- Tape measure
- String line
- Drill and ½" × 10" drill bit
- ½" nut driver bit (for ½" hex-head lag bolts)
- 5-gallon buckets
- 2'–3' level
- Speed square
- Paintbrush or roller
- Miter saw
- Tarp
- 6' ladder

## MATERIALS

- Sixteen 50-lb bags of concrete
- Four 6" × 6" metal standoff post bases
- Four 6" × 6" × 8' rough cedar posts
- Twenty-four ½" malleable washers
- Three cans latex-based spray paint for galvanized steel (do not use regular alkyd-based paint, which chemically reacts with the galvanized zinc coating and will peel off)
- Six 2" × 6" × 12' cedar boards (or use 2" × 8"s for a bigger, bolder structure), cut to the following dimensions:
  - Two cut to 11' 5" with vertical 45° mitered edges
  - Two cut to 11' 2"
  - Six cut to 44"
- Four 2" × 6" × 16' cedar boards cut to the following dimensions:
  - Two cut to 14' with vertical 45° mitered edges
  - Two cut to 12' 6"
  - Eight cut to 6"
- One 1-lb box of 1" screws (to attach joist hangers)
- Sixteen 2" × 6" joist hangers
- 1 gallon of wood stain
- Eight 3½" lag bolts
- Four 10" through bolts
- 14' × 12' shade fabric
- Butterfly clips or staples (optional, if adding shade fabric)

STEP 1: **Select an area and collect your materials:** Choose a location that could benefit from a little shade and that will add impact to the yard. The back of the house is a great location because it works as an extension of the interior. Select your preferred lumber: pressure-treated, cedar and redwood are my go-tos. I used Western red cedar posts that had been planed down to give it a modern, sleek look.

STEP 2: **Dig the post holes:** Dig out four 18 × 18 × 24-inch deep holes. For this project, I poured a brand-new pad, so the footings became part of the patio. If you are placing a structure over an existing concrete patio, a different post base can be used by drilling into the concrete.

STEP 3: **Pour the concrete:** Mix the concrete in a 5-gallon bucket. Fill the hole with concrete and level off with the finished grade.

STEP 4: **Set the post bases:** The post bases allow the lumber to sit about 1 inch above the grade, keeping them drier and stronger for longer. Set the post base in the wet concrete and make sure they are plumb to each other by using a mason's line. The bottom of the metal plate should sit at the level of the grade, making the top of the metal plate sit proud of the grade. Let the post bases set up overnight.

**STEP 5:** **Set the posts:** Install the 8-foot 6 × 6 posts by screwing them into the post bases with the screws and washers that come with the post bases.

**STEP 6:** **Paint the bolts and washers:** Paint all the bolts and malleable washers with latex-based paint. Let dry.

**STEP 7:** **Attach the beams:** Now that your posts are set up, start with your outside frame. Since this structure is finished at roughly 8 feet tall, we lined up the lumber flush to the top on one end. Use a level to verify that the beams are being attached level. With a friend, attach one of your miter-cut 11-foot-5-inch 2 × 6 beams, overrunning the sides by 2 inches, or right where the miter-cut edge starts. Secure one of your 11-foot-2-inch 2 × 6-inch beams with two through bolts stacked vertically and a malleable washer on each side to attach both the 11-foot-5-inch 2 × 6 and the 11-foot-2-inch 2 × 6 boards on either side of the 6 × 6-inch post. Be sure to predrill the holes. Repeat this step on the other end, and then on the other side. Next, attach your mitered 14-foot 2 × 6-inch piece with malleable washers and 3½-inch lag bolts so that it is perpendicular to the first beams. Repeat on the other end and then on the other side to complete the outside frame.

STEP 8: **Attach the crossbeams:** Attach the running 12-foot 2 × 6-inch beams starting at 44 inches in from the 14-foot 2 × 6s with joist hangers, perpendicular to the 11-foot-2-inch 2 × 6-inch beam. There should be at least three rows. I wanted to keep this structure very simple, so it has only two running beams. Next, attach all your 44-inch 2 × 6-inch cross beams with joist hangers to the long running beams, spaced 49 inches from each other. This completes the basics of your structure. Again, gussets can be added to reinforce the long runs of lumber to prevent sagging in the future (not shown for this structure).

STEP 9: **Stain the wood:** Select a stain and a sealer to protect your wood and add color. I used a very dark brown/gray that references the metal. Add a tarp to any finished areas below to keep them clean. Alternatively, you can stain all the wood before assembly if you prefer.

STEP 10: **Optional:** Add light shade: You can attach a shade fabric with simple butterfly clips or staples to give you shade and a softer light. Canvas can be bought in 6- and 12-foot lengths and can be overlapped over beams to give you a seamless look. For this project, I needed to cut only 14 inches of canvas off a 12-foot roll.

# CHAPTER 5

# OUTDOOR GAMES

## WHERE THE FUN IS

Playing games during social events brings people together and strengthens relationships. In today's world, with everyone always plugged in on some sort of device, it's refreshing to have a physical activity that you can do with your friends and family to share some laughs. Yards with permanent game features instantly become an excuse to have people visit, hang out and spend time outside.

Not only are games fun, but they also give purpose to yards both large and small. Most people have much more yard than they actually use, so installing game features is a great way to give a yard lawn character and extend the usefulness of your space. This chapter will focus on some ways you can bring games into your outdoor space, such as horseshoes, volleyball, badminton, bocce and cornhole. You'll learn how to build your own bocce court (page 61) and a dry erase scoreboard (page 68) for when things get competitive.

# GAME OPTIONS FOR SOCIAL GATHERINGS

Games and activities can have permanent presence in the yard, such as the Bocce Ball Court project (page 61), or be adapted to a space on an as-needed basis. An open, level lawn can provide a great space for volleyball, Frisbee, "Viking chess" (tossing wooden blocks) and other free-form games. Here are a few options for your yard:

**Horseshoes.** This classic game is an easy addition to any yard that has the space, but keep in mind running children and glass windows. This game is best played on the far side of the lawn, where misthrown horseshoes will miss any built features. Two 36 × 48-inch sandbox pits spaced 40 feet apart, stake to stake, is a good size for playing horseshoes.

**Volleyball and badminton.** If you have a large space such as an open field and lawn, then you have a great opportunity to put up a volleyball or badminton net. I am the least athletic of my family and I can still hold my own in a game of volleyball, and when I can't, it's still fun.

**Bocce.** This Italian pastime is a great casual game that can be played in an open space or on a court. The courts are the official way to play and take up a decent amount of space. However, even when it is not being used, a bocce ball court offers a pleasing aesthetic to an outdoor space.

**Cornhole.** This classic game of throwing colored beanbags onto boards spaced 30 feet apart on the center of the hole has been around at tailgate parties for a long time. It has really gained a lot of popularity at house parties and outdoor events in general. With four bags for each side and two 2 × 4-foot wooden boards, it's mobile and easy to set up and store.

# BOCCE BALL COURT

LEVEL: INTERMEDIATE
COST: $$
TIME COMMITMENT: 1–2 WEEKENDS
PROFESSIONALS NEEDED: NONE
DIMENSIONS: 6' × 29'

Out of all the outdoor games, bocce ball is one of my favorites and is a cool feature in a yard. Not only is it fun to play, but it also adds another area of interest to a backyard and organizes a space for plantings and other useful features, such as benches and tables. Regulation bocce ball courts vary from 8 to 14 feet wide and 60 to 90 feet long, which can be hard to achieve in your standard residential neighborhood, so consider creating a half court or something that fits your space. The dimensions may vary depending on the space that you have, but I wouldn't go smaller than 29 by 6 feet, which is a half court. With simple materials and construction techniques, it is possible to put together your own court in as little as a weekend. The mix for the bocce court comes in gray, sand, pure white, oyster shell and more, or you can use decomposed granite, which is a little more affordable.

(continued)

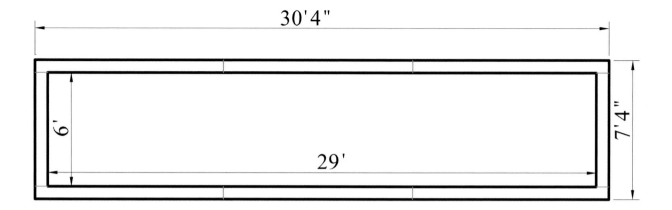

## TOOLS

- Measuring tape
- Mason's twine and stakes
- Flat-edge shovel
- Wheelbarrow
- Leveling rake or 2" × 4"
- Hose with adjustable nozzle
- Walk-behind compactor plate (can be rented at any big box store)
- Paintbrush (optional, if applying wood stain)
- 4' level
- Electric drill (battery drills will die quickly) and ½" × 10" wood drill bit
- Mini sledgehammer
- Hand tamper

## MATERIALS

- Can of marking spray
- 4 cubic yards of base material
- Eight 6" × 8" × 10' cedar, redwood or pressure-treated lumber
- One 6" × 8" × 12' cedar, redwood or pressure-treated lumber, cut in half
- Pressure-treatment solution (optional)
- Protective wood stain (optional)
- Eight 12" timber ties
- Tape
- Twenty-two ½" rebar cut to 2' long
- 4 cubic yards of bocce court mix or decomposed granite
- 1 cubic yard of mason's sand

**STEP 1:** **Select an area:** This is a big feature, but unlike an overhead structure, you won't be using it daily, so you may want to tuck it into a corner or the back of the property, depending on how big your yard is. Don't place it so far from the entertaining areas that people feel isolated if they are going to play. Choose an area that people can move in and out of and still feel like they are part of the party when they are playing. I chose an area near the fireplace and plan to add a scoreboard for players and viewers to gather around.

**STEP 2:** **Mark the court:** Use marking spray to rough out the dimensions of the court. I used the fence line as my parallel guide to mark and spray out a court 7 feet 8 inches wide and 31 feet long, for a finished court of 6 feet wide and approximately 29 feet long. I spaced the court 4 feet inside the property so I had room for plants and seating. (If the ground is very dry, mist it with a hose first for better adhesion of the spray paint.)

**STEP 3:** **Excavate:** Secure a string line on both sides to give you a reliable reference for digging. Then use a flat-edge shovel to dig down 8 inches. I marked the course extra wide and long so that I could fit the lumber and gravel backfill.

STEP 4: **Build and compact the base:** Shovel the base material into a wheelbarrow and start dropping it off on the far side of the court, spreading it and moving your way down as you go. You want a total of 4 inches of compacted base, which is about 4 cubic yards. Use a leveling rake or a piece of 2 × 4 to roughly level out the gravel as you work your way down.

Compacting is an important step because your court can settle over time and create an uneven surface, which would be bad for accuracy and direction when playing. You can compact with a hand tamper, but it would take forever. For best results, rent a plate compactor from a local hardware store or rental center. You can get one for between $40 and $70 per day. This machine is not as scary as it looks; it starts and drives just like a lawn mower with a punch. Before you compact the base of the court, mist down the area with a hose to keep the dust down and to help the compaction process. Drive it up and down the court area in rows, compacting the base as you go.

STEP 5: **Prepare the lumber:** Depending on what's available in your area, you will likely have the choices of cedar or pressure-treated lumber and maybe redwood or Alaskan yellow cedar. All are good choices, but pressure-treated is the best in terms of longevity as it is chemically treated to resist rot and insects. I used Alaskan yellow cedar, which is naturally resistant to rot and insects. Although this lumber is rated for ground contact, I applied a coat of pressure-treatment solution to the bottom and stained the other sides of the lumber with a protecting color stain to extend the longevity of the lumber even further.

STEP 6: **Set the lumber:** Use a mason's line attached to a stake to mark out the 7 × 30-foot area again and place the string 8 inches above the top of the base. Create a bed for the lumber to sit on with mason's sand about 2 inches wider on either side. Compact with a hand tamper. Reference the mason's line to level off each of the pieces of lumber. Place three 10-foot 6 × 8s on the long sides and tuck one 6-foot 6 × 8 perpendicular to the long sides on either end of the court. Use a level and a speed square to ensure the frame is level and square.

**STEP 7:** **Install side supports:** Install two 12-inch timber ties on each corner to secure the 6-foot end pieces to the vertical lengths of wood on the inside.

**STEP 8:** **Drill the holes:** Using a ½-inch drill bit and an electric drill, make three holes in each 10-foot piece of lumber and two holes in each 6-foot piece of lumber. For the 10-foot pieces, drill a hole 6 inches in from each edge and one in the center. For the 6-foot pieces, drill a hole 6 inches in from each edge. Use a piece of tape to mark a depth of 8 inches on the drill bit so you don't drill down into the base, dulling the bit.

**STEP 9:** **Secure with rebar:** Fit one of the 2-foot pieces of rebar in the predrilled hole and use a mini sledgehammer to drive through the lumber, the base and all the way into the ground. Continue until all the predrilled sides are done. This will help secure the lumber from being pushed out of place.

**STEP 10:** **Add bocce ball mix:** Bring in wheelbarrows of bocce ball mix. Spread the mix so that it is 3 to 4 inches deep. Use a 2 × 4 to screed (roughly level) the mix and then check the level with an actual level.

**STEP 11:** **Mist the bocce mix:** Use a garden hose to mist the bocce mix, which will help compact it.

**STEP 12:** **Compact the bocce mix:** Use the walk-behind plate compactor to compact the surface, mist it again and run over it two or three more times. Invite your friends over, crack open a beer and toss some balls!

# MAGNETIC BOCCE COURT COVER

Some areas in the yard collect more leaf litter than others. If you place your court under a tree or have a lot of potential debris, consider adding a cover. The concept for this cover is pretty simple and uses canvas, magnets and steel to keep your court clean and tidy and ready for guests when they visit. Spray a protective coat of metal spray paint on eight 1½-inch × 10-foot pieces of steel and attach them to the edge of your bocce court. I spaced mine about 1 inch below the top edge of the wood, so it appears to be a cool design detail. Cut your canvas to size with enough fabric so that you can fold over the edges and sew ½-inch neodymium magnets into the hem on all sides. Neodymium rare earth magnets are the strongest magnets in the world. I spaced them every 16 inches or so and put two on each corner edge. This concept can be used for a lot of other projects that need a casual and attractive cover, as well.

# SCOREBOARD WALL

**LEVEL: BEGINNER TO INTERMEDIATE**
**COST: $$**
**TIME COMMITMENT: 1 DAY**
**PROFESSIONALS NEEDED: NONE**
**DIMENSIONS: 6'6" × 6"**

This is a fun project that assembles easily and is aesthetically pleasing as well. The porcelain tiles are framed in lumber to create a scoreboard or drawing board to keep track of points. You simply add some dry erase markers, an eraser and some erasing solution. If your tile is fairly porous, consider using a sealer so the tiles don't absorb the dry erase markers. Don't limit yourself to keeping score; consider installing one of these as a noteboard or menu board for a kitchen space.

## TOOLS

- Table saw (optional: you can buy 2" × 2" posts instead of splitting)
- Router and bit
- Chop saw or miter saw
- Speed square
- Drill and bits

## MATERIALS

- Two 4" × 4" × 8' pressure-treated posts
- Two 2" × 6" cedar posts, cut to 71" (just under 6')
- One 2" × 4" post, split in half and cut to get two 2" × 1¾" × 71" boards (or use two 2" × 2" × 6' posts if you don't have a table saw)
- One 2" × 6" × 8' post, cut to 6' 6"
- Six 60-lb bags of concrete (for posts)
- 1 box of 3" exterior screws
- Three 2' × 2' light-colored porcelain tiles with finish (they are actually 23½" squares)
- One 1" × 4" cedar board, split in half and cut to 23½" for a total of two 2" × 1¾" × 23½" pieces
- Two 2" × 6" × 6" corbels (made by cutting a 2" × 6" at a 45° angle)
- Two 1½" × 23½" metal bars (or use lumber)
- Dry erase markers and eraser
- Four 1" self-piercing screws (or predrill)

STEP 1: **Select a location and set the posts:** Choose an area that is easily accessible to your bocce ball court or other game, or a spot where you can use a whiteboard for making notes. I choose to place the base of the scoreboard at roughly countertop height so it's easy to see and the dry erase pens will be easy to grab!

Dig the holes 20 inches deep and 1 foot wide, mix three bags of concrete per post and set the posts so that at least 18 inches are embedded in the concrete. Make sure the posts are plumb and measure 71 inches from inside to inside.

STEP 2: **Create the top and bottom frame:** Take one of your 71-inch 2 × 6-inch boards and attach the 71-inch 2 × 2-inch board so it is flush to one side; repeat this step so that you have two separate units. Use exterior 3-inch screws to secure on each end, about 2 feet in on either side.

**STEP 3:** **Attach the frame to the posts:** Measure 36 inches up from the ground level and attach one of the units made in the last step so that it lines up with the back of the 4 x 4-inch post. Use a speed square to make sure you have a 90° angle. It should protrude about 1½ inches in front of the 4 × 4 post. Then space the top one so you have an approximately 23½-inch gap between the boards. Your porcelain tiles are 23½ inches tall and will fit in this frame.

**STEP 4:** **Add the corbels:** Use the miter saw to cut two 2 x 6 x 6 corbels. Predrill one hole about 1½ inches up from the bottom; this will tie into the 4 x 4 post. Predrill another hole at an angle about 1 inch from the top. This will tie into the bottom horizontal board.

**STEP 5:** **Place the porcelain tiles:** Now take your three tiles and place them so they rest on the bottom 71-inch 2 × 6-inch board and against the vertical supports you just attached. Space the tiles so you have approximately ¼ inch between the two center tiles.

**STEP 6:** **Drill holes:** Take the two 23½-inch metal bars and use a metal drill bit to drill holes on the bottom and top center about ¾ inch in from each side.

STEP 7: **Secure the tiles:** Place one metal bar over the space to cover the gap and attach each one with 1-inch screws to the 71-inch 2 × 2-inch vertical frames on the top and bottom. Then repeat on the other gap.

STEP 8: **Secure the wood frame to the posts:** Take your two 2 × 1¾ × 23½ split cedar boards and flank them on the far side of the tile. Secure them to the 4 × 4 posts with 3-inch screws. This will hold your tiles in place.

STEP 9: **Router:** Measure ¾ inch in from the edge of the bottom 71-inch 2 × 6-inch piece and 2 feet from the center on either side for a 4-foot-long space. Use a router and a bit to create a 4-foot-long ½-inch dado groove. This will house the dry erase markers.

STEP 10: **Final touches:** Use the 6-foot-6-inch 2 × 6-inch lumber and attach with 3-inch screws to each 4 × 4-inch post to overhang evenly. Now try out your calligraphy skills and invite your friends over for a competitive game!

# STONE, LUMBER, METAL AND MASONRY, OH MY!

## THE ABCS OF EXTERIOR MATERIALS

Building with basic materials can be as complicated or as simple as you make it. This section breaks down common landscape construction materials and gives you the pros and cons of each type, so when you start planning and building you can have a leg up in the game. I like to say that on average materials are at least one-third of the construction cost, so if you're familiar with your options, you can make educated decisions that will affect your bottom line.

You will notice that I use the term *hardscape* a lot in this section. Basically, hardscape is any permanent or semipermanent material that is not living and is not easily changed. Examples of hardscape materials include concrete, natural stones, pavers, tiles and lumber. Hardscape materials tend to be more expensive and longer lasting than *softscape* items, which include garden mulch, plants, lawns and anything that is living or that can decompose relatively quickly. This section covers hardscape materials; Section Three focuses on softscape materials.

There are endless options when it comes to hardscape materials. Choices will vary from region to region and even popularity of use, depending on the environment, climate and regional style. The only way you can break out of the "ordinary box" is by understanding what is available and how to manipulate those materials to make your projects custom and unique. When I first started building, I had no idea what type of lumber was common to use for outdoor projects and why. But now that I am empowered with that information, I can focus my energy on other things, like how to use those materials to maximize creativity.

## COST, LONGEVITY AND MAINTENANCE

Choosing the right hardscape materials can be tricky, because you have to balance your preferences with your budget and your maintenance needs. Of course, everyone wants the lowest-maintenance yard possible, but that doesn't always translate to better. I've seen yards covered in concrete . . . it must be easy to maintain, if you can stand it! It's all about striking a balance, and understanding the options in materials is the key to choosing what is right for you and your yard.

Your budget is also a big factor when looking at exterior landscape materials. And of course, everyone wants the most affordable yard, but this is not always the highest priority for your design, as you might end up unhappy with the results in the long run. For example, you can build the same deck out of Douglas fir or ipe. Ipe costs at least three to four times more, but will last five times longer than Douglas fir, looks good over the long run and requires less upkeep. Douglas fir, on the other hand, tends to warp and twist and is very susceptible to rot and insects. Douglas fir also requires a lot more attention and upkeep to stay functional; it just can't compare to the quality of ipe lumber. There are material choices in between that can balance the budget versus longevity argument, and that is why knowing your options is key.

## PROPERTY VALUE AND MATERIAL CHOICES

If you are interested in the resale value of your home, then pick basic or traditional materials that will appeal to the greatest number of people when it comes to permanent or long-lasting structures. Leave that orange and pink tile combo for your forever home . . . or maybe forget it altogether! Pavers, natural stone and concrete have a universal appeal to a wider range of potential buyers.

In the end, however, the materials you choose are not as important (as long as they're within the realm of "normal") as the extra functions that add value to your home. Hardscape is expensive to install but long lasting and low maintenance, which are both important features for potential buyers.

# CHAPTER 6

# STONE FOR EVERY STYLE OF YARD
## NATURE'S BUILDING BLOCKS

Most landscapes have some sort of natural stone element, whether it's a gravel patio, a flagstone path or well-positioned boulders. It's hard to beat the character and beauty of this durable and classic material. Stone is so versatile—from natural-edge flagstone, to cut stone tiles, to loose gravel, boulders and manufactured veneers—that it can literally fit in with any style. You see stone in modern gardens and in rustic gardens, in expensive yards and in affordable yards. This chapter will present an overview of natural stone, its various applications, and costs and things to consider when working with it. Several projects, including a dry-set garden path (page 78), a flagstone patio (page 82), a dry creek bed (page 86) and a pebble carpet mosaic (page 90), will show you just how easy it is to highlight stone in your landscape renovation, as its timeless beauty retains its value for current and future homeowners. Natural stone is harvested from different quarries all over the world, supplying a wide variety of colors, textures and strengths. But because stone is sold and shipped by weight, it can get quite expensive, especially if your selection is coming from a far-off location. Most stone yards carry a handful of locally sourced stone, so that will be the most affordable option, plus they will most likely tie into your surrounding environment best.

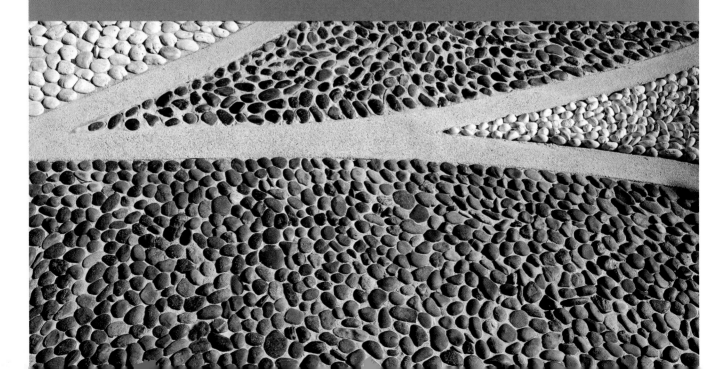

## OVERVIEW OF STONE

A local stone yard will showcase many styles of product in one location. You might need to drive out of town just a little bit to find a stone yard, but the savings on bulk orders will be worth it. Stone yards are great resources for information about the products, have wide selections and also offer delivery options, which you'll need for your heavy order. You can also find basic products and a handful of specialty products at hardware stores, landscape supply stores, tile stores and big box stores. And don't forget to look in your own yard: your soil might be hiding a plethora of small boulders, so consider incorporating them as you find them when digging for your different projects.

## EASE OF USE

Working with stone can be an art, from fitting together flagstones to placing boulders. Sometimes heavy machinery is needed to assist transporting, delivering and placing the materials, which can make it challenging. Moving, cutting and placing stone is labor-intensive, and the process can be repetitive and tiring, but the final results are worth it and will permanently enhance your exterior spaces.

## CONSIDERATIONS

**WEIGHT:** Consider the weight on the car if you're planning on transporting stone. I usually budget $100 to have it delivered instead of putting the wear and tear on my vehicle.

**TIMELINE:** From cutting, chiseling, to just loading a wheelbarrow full of gravel, handling stone is heavy work and not a quick process. Factor in work breaks and being sore the next day.

**DIY OR HIRE:** Consider that you can make expensive mistakes when you do it yourself. For example, if you use thinset to veneer stones to a surface and find you've made a mistake, it's almost impossible to salvage the material if it has set or hardened. Starting over from scratch or chiseling mortar off the back of a tile would never happen on a construction site, as it's not cost effective.

**MACHINES:** Bringing a skid steer to the location will up the cost but save you a lot in time. If you plan on moving a lot of boulders or loose stone, it may be worth renting one for a day (plus, it's a lot of fun!).

## COST

So many factors can affect the cost of a project, from how the material is sourced to how far it's being transported to how much is available. Generally speaking, dry-set or loose applications are more affordable when it comes to installation; wet-set applications, meaning the material is adhered to a hard surface with mortar or thinset, are usually more expensive. You can save money and achieve the same aesthetic if you consider using architectural stone veneer products, which are concrete-based materials made to look like stone.

# USING STONE IN THE LANDSCAPE

There are a ton of options when using boulders, landscape gravel, flagstone, architectural stone veneer and stacked stone veneer. I love using natural stone for patios, paths and veneers. Nothing quite compares to the raw beauty of stone.

## BOULDERS: $–$$

**Description:** Boulders help naturalize and organize a space. But remember, the bigger the boulder, the harder it is to move around, and the more expensive it is. I never order boulders bigger than 2½ to 3 feet in diameter without ordering machinery to place them. I consider a stone to be a boulder if it is at least 1½ feet in diameter. Boulders work nicely for natural retaining, accents and edging.

**Cost factors:** Boulders can be sold by the rough size or by weight. The parent material of the rock greatly affects the weight. So if you choose a lighter stone, you get more bang for your buck.

## LANDSCAPE GRAVEL/COBBLE: $–$$

**Description:** Gravel comes in a variety of sizes, from ⅛ to 1½ inches, with ⅜ and ¾ inches being the most widely used sizes for residential paths and patios. There are round rocks that I refer to as "cobble," with diameters ranging from 2 to 12 inches, which are better suited for decorative, not walking, surfaces, such as a creek bed or in garden areas. Decomposed granite is the finest "gravel" that you can find. It is basically broken-down pieces of granite about the size of large sand particles and it compacts to make a solid walking surface. Decomposed granite is great for patios, paths and gardens, but be sure to put this affordable material at the back of a house, as it will track in on people's shoes.

**Cost factors:** Landscape gravel is usually sold by the ton, by the scoop or by the yard. Common gravels are pretty affordable and offer a lot of bang for your buck. When you start looking at decorative stones like Mexican beach pebble, it can get pricey fast. The price can vary greatly depending on the type of stone, its color and where it came from.

## FLAGSTONE: $$$

**Description:** Flagstone comes in a variety of thicknesses, shapes and colors and is a great choice for many hardscape applications, from paths to fireplace veneers. Natural-edge flagstone is popular for a more rustic look, while cut edges can give the stone a more modern style. It is one of the more expensive materials to purchase and work with, but it adds a lot of value to a space and the maintenance is minimal.

**Cost factors:** Flagstone is usually sold by the pallet, by weight or by piece. The best way to estimate the cost for your project is to figure out your square footage and select a thickness. I recommend a 2-inch thickness for any dry-set application to prevent the stones from breaking under the pressure of foot traffic.

**MORTAR-SET FLAGSTONE.** This is also known as wet-set flagstone because the stone is set on wet thinset and adhered to a hard concrete base. Usually a thin stone is used to minimize elevation change, and since it's used as a veneer, it doesn't need to be as strong. If you need to add more than ¼ inch of thinset, use mortar to raise it to the height you need and then use thinset on the stone and substrate surface.

**DRY-SET FLAGSTONE.** This type of flagstone is typically less expensive and more informal than mortar set. It requires setting thick slabs of flagstone on a compacted substrate, such as gravel or soil. I recommend 2-inch-thick stones on a compacted base. The style of spacing can vary a lot, depending on the design aesthetic. I typically like to chisel the edges to match up the sides of the stone and space them about 2¾ inches apart at most. The more consistent the spacing, the more professional the job will look. Or for a more informal garden path, these can and should be a lot more casually spaced. Use thick slabs and space them based on a normal walking gait (see page 80).

## ARCHITECTURAL/CONCRETE STONE VENEER: $–$$

**Description:** Stone can be expensive, especially when covering a large area, so sometimes stone veneer, which looks and feels like real stone but is made of a concrete material, is used instead. The benefits of concrete stone are that it is lighter in weight and easier on the budget. In fact, you can estimate that it will weigh half of what real stone weighs and cost half the price! Plus, there is a wide variety of options in all kinds of patterns and colors. Steer clear of the budget options with manufactured stone, though, and go with quality architectural stone, as the differences in quality are more obvious with stone veneers.

**Cost factors:** Concrete stone veneers are usually sold by the panel or box and prices can vary depending on quality. Again, always choose a top brand because you will see the difference on a veneer.

## NATURAL STACKED STONE VENEER: $$–$$$

**Description:** These are natural stones that are cut and manufactured as individual pieces or panels. They are typically used in vertical applications, such as on walls, siding and columns. These cut stones come in a wide variety of colors, patterns and textures.

**Cost factors:** Natural stacked stone veneers can be costly, because of the additional processes of cutting and manufacturing the panels. Save money by looking for discontinued stock at stone yards, but make sure there is enough for your project plus an extra 20 percent available (every project needs a buffer). Also consider purchasing panels rather than individually placed pieces to save on labor costs.

# DRY-SET NATURAL GARDEN PATH

**LEVEL: BEGINNER**
**COST: $$**
**TIME COMMITMENT: 1 DAY**
**PROFESSIONALS NEEDED: NONE**
**DIMENSIONS: 12' × 3'**

Natural stone is timeless and universally appreciated, and this project will soften your landscape and add value to your home. A dry-set flagstone path creates direction and brings a lot of character and visual impact to a yard. Its solid and natural form is a great complement to surrounding vegetation. You'll be happy on rainy days not to have to tromp along a muddy path anymore!

BEFORE

## TOOLS

- Safety goggles
- Gloves
- Shovel
- Rake
- Hose and multispray nozzle
- Hand tamper
- 2'–3' level
- Torpedo level

## MATERIALS

- ¾ ton of natural-edge stone (seven 14–18" wide × 18–24" long × 1½–2½" thick pieces)
- Can of marking spray
- Two 2-cubic-foot bags of decomposed granite or masonry sand
- Four 2-cubic-foot bags of base material (or compact existing dirt)
- Six 2-cubic-foot bags of mulch, wood chips, gravel or other filler

**STEP 1:** **Select your stone:** Look for thick 1½- to 2½-inch slabs with relatively smooth surfaces and rough natural edges. Thinner flagstone will crack under the pressure of walking with this style of path. The color should either match or complement existing or proposed materials in the landscape. Natural-edge stone offers a more relaxed, country, cottage or rustic feel, while cut-edge stone will read modern, clean, organized and contemporary.

**STEP 2:** **Select the location and prep:** Select an area that is either already used as a path or make a garden more interesting by intersecting a path through it. Mark it out with marking spray. (If the ground is very dry, mist it with a hose first for better adhesion.) With a shovel, dig out roughly 1 inch below the finished grade and a little wider on each side. This is just enough to drop the flagstone in lightly. Since the ground is going to be raised around it with mulch, the flagstone can sit proud of the ground when in place. If digging in very sandy or clay soil or in an area that freezes, dig down 2 to 4 inches deep and 2 inches wider than each stone and add base material. Rake the area smooth.

2

STEP 3: **Lay out the stone and test:** "Field fit" the pieces of flagstone with the spacing you desire. Practice walking over to match the placement of stones to your natural gait and move the stones accordingly. If members of your household have a big height difference (for example, my mom is 4 foot 11 inches and my dad is 6 foot), find the average gait difference and compromise. Since this is an informal garden path, no cutting or chiseling is necessary.

STEP 4: **Add the base:** Pick up one stone at a time. Add a few shovelfuls of decomposed granite or masonry sand, lightly mist with a garden hose to help settle the material and compact it with a hand tamper. I used decomposed granite.

STEP 5: **Lay out the stone and level:** Reset each stone in place in its newly dug out and compacted hole. Adjust each stone, and check to see if it's level in both directions. If it is not sitting flat, add more base or cut and fill until the stone is secure. If your path is flat, use a 2-foot level to level the stones to each other, or if on a slight slope, step them down to each other. Step on each stone to see if it rocks around, and if so, add scoops of masonry sand and spread until it levels.

**STEP 6:** **Test your work:** You can test your handiwork by stepping on it. If it moves a lot, then you need to keep working on it by cutting and filling and leveling.

**STEP 7:** **Check your level again and fill in:** Now that the stones are set they should still be sitting 1½ to 2 inches taller than the ground. Use your torpedo level to check the level once again and to make sure they are secure and then fill in the surrounding area with mulch, wood chips, gravel or other filler to finish off the informal garden path. Now enjoy trotting across your new path to enjoy your yard!

# WET-SET FLAGSTONE PATIO ON GRADE

**LEVEL: INTERMEDIATE TO ADVANCED**
**COST: $$–$$$**
**TIME COMMITMENT: 2 WEEKENDS**
**PROFESSIONALS NEEDED: NONE**
**DIMENSIONS: VARIES, DEPENDING ON YOUR SPACE**
**(THIS SPACE IS 17' × 16')**

Wet setting loose flagstone pieces is the best way to stabilize a flagstone patio, as it mitigates shifting and moving because it thickens the width and levels the pieces. However, it is a lot more work than dry setting and can be a little more challenging. Wet set basically means the flagstone is set with wet mortar. For this project, the flagstone pieces are set on compacted ground with wide grout borders to allow for filler stones, creating an informal, rustic look.

## TOOLS

- Shovel
- Measuring tape
- Mason's hammer
- Wheelbarrow
- 5-gallon bucket
- Mason's line
- Rubber mallet
- Trowel
- 3' level
- Torpedo level (mini level)

## MATERIALS

- One pallet of 1½"–2" thick flagstone
- 2½ tons or 2 cubic yards of C-mix (pea gravel and sand mix)
- Ten to twelve 94-lb bags of Portland cement (bagged concrete can be substituted for the C-mix and Portland)
- Five 50-lb bags of thinset
- 1½ cubic yards of 1"–2" rounded stone

**STEP 1:** **Select your location and dig:** Patios should be seen as gathering spaces, so choose an area that you know you will use. For this job, I selected the area in front of the fireplace, as I know people will use it. Grade the area so that your flagstone will sit flush with any existing patio floor or other features (if present). I dug 3 to 4 inches down so that the 1½- to 2-inch flagstone could sit flush to the fireplace's existing concrete pad when backfilled with concrete.

**STEP 2:** **Lay out and cut:** Lay out the stones and try to line up the edges as best you can; use a mason's hammer to make adjustments. Since this is more of an informal patio, I let the grout spaces go wide, minimizing cuts and maximizing the materials while still trying to match edges. Lay out the entire patio at one time.

**STEP 3:** **Mix the concrete and set the line:** Using a wheelbarrow, mix around 26 shovelfuls of C-mix with half of a 94-pound bag of Portland cement. Also mix thinset in a 5-gallon bucket. Set a mason's line across the work area to set the finished height of the patio.

**STEP 4:** **Place the flagstone:** Remove a piece of stone and shovel the concrete to fill underneath thick and wide. The concrete should be higher than the patio level, as it will press out under the pressure of the stone and this gives you wiggle room to level the stone by tapping it with a rubber mallet. If you are dealing with large stones, get a buddy to help you lower the stone onto the concrete. Once you fit the stone, pull it off evenly and use a trowel to spread a ¼-inch layer of thinset along the bottom and then place the stone back down. This is what really holds the stone to the concrete, as thinset is more adhesive than concrete. Adjust and check with a level once more. This patio also included a 3- by 7½-foot pebble mosaic in the center and space was left empty for it. If you choose not to include a mosaic, then continue filling the patio in from one side to the next.

**STEP 5:** **Clean and repeat:** After the stone is level, trim out all the extra extruding concrete with a trowel and use it for the next stone. Make sure the stones are level to each other. Continue this process until a section or the entire patio is complete, mixing up more concrete and thinset as needed.

**STEP 6:** **Add the rounded stone:** After all the flagstone pieces are set, use a shovel or a bucket to drop rocks in between the flagstones; some may kick out at first but over time they will settle in as they are compacted whenever people walk on them. This patio will last the lifetime of the home, and it adds character and function in such a pleasing way!

## SET A FLAGSTONE PATIO ON A CONCRETE PAD

If you already have an existing concrete pad, you can set a new flagstone floor on top. Select any flat stone or tile, as long as you have the room to add without going higher than your weep screed or your door height; from ½ to 1½ inches is ideal. Straight-edge stones are easier to line up and get consistent grout spaces and lean toward a contemporary look, while natural-edge flagstone is a classic look for many spaces. Clean off your surface of grime and dirt. Starting in one corner, lay out all of your stone, working across the space. Cut or shape your flagstone as needed with a tile saw and/or a mason's hammer. Some people use a grinder, but I don't recommend this for beginners as this tool is inherently dangerous.

Pick up one stone at a time and place a layer of thinset. If you need to raise the level higher than ¼ to ½ inch, then add type S mortar to give you some height and help you level the stones. Add a thin layer of thinset to the back of the stone and then place it and check the level. Make sure you direct the level to slope away from your structure and use a rubber mallet to tap the stones into place, leveling them to each other and the space. You will likely get overflow mortar on the sides, so clean this up with a trowel and work your way across the space.

## PEBBLE PATHWAY

Pebbles are an easy and affordable solution for a functional and aesthetically pleasing pathway. Loose pea gravel like this is best for a secondary path rather than a main path because it pushes out a little as you walk on it. This is fine for casual use, but would probably drive you nuts if it were used for your main entrance.

To create this path, we dug out the pathway and covered it with landscape fabric, pinning it down with landscape staples and tucking it under the large stones used for edging. The landscape fabric helps prevent weeds from sprouting up and keeps the gravel from being pushed into the soil and lost over time. Dump the gravel by the wheelbarrow, spread it out with a rake and you're done. Periodically you may have to add a little gravel and pick out some weeds, but overall this gravel path is a simple, budget-friendly and low-maintenance way to create a sense of movement in your yard.

# DRY CREEK BED

**LEVEL: BEGINNER**
**COST: $$**
**TIME COMMITMENT: 1–2 WEEKENDS**
**PROFESSIONALS NEEDED: NONE**
**DIMENSIONS: 4' × 60' (FANS OUT TO 10' WIDE AT END)**

Dividing a yard with a dry creek bed creates dimension and offers a form for other landscape elements to play off. If you can tie in your existing downspouts or else direct water into it to infiltrate back into the ground, Mother Nature will love it, too. This unique feature also creates a relaxing and aesthetically pleasing focal point and a place for kids to play.

A dry creek bed can enhance almost any yard, front or back, and it works in both drought-tolerant and lush landscapes alike. Your creek bed should follow the natural grade of the land, so place it where water naturally travels. Take note next time it rains and follow the direction of the water to see where the water naturally travels; you can then either enhance the existing flow of water or redirect it to fit your yard's aesthetic.

Having a little drop in terms of grade can be helpful, but it's not necessary because you can manipulate the grade by hand. In fact, if you have a decent slope of 15 degrees or less (any more than that gets tricky), you can have a lot of fun following the grade and redirecting the flow with boulders and making wide switchbacks.

I like placing dry creek beds as an edging or using them to divide elements. The edge of a lawn with a planting space is a good line to follow. Dry creek beds also look great winding through a garden space. If you have an issue with water on your property, having a system like this is hugely beneficial in directing and slowing down the flow if needed. However, a dry creek bed does not have to be functional to bring beauty and interest to your yard, and the upkeep is minimal.

## TOOLS

- Gloves
- Hose and multispray nozzle
- Breaker bar
- Utility knife
- Spade shovel
- Wheelbarrow
- Mallet or hammer (for landscape staples)

## MATERIALS

- Three to five 1½–3' boulders
- 2½ tons of 5–8" stones
- 1½ tons of 3–5" stones
- 2–3 tons of 1–2" gravel
- Can of marking spray
- 300 sq ft 6'-wide roll of landscape fabric
- 2 boxes (75-count) of landscape staples

STEP 1: **Select your boulders, stone and gravel:** Try to match or complement the colors of the different stones. It's okay to have variety, but similar colors will look more natural. Boulders are your accents and anchor areas for turns in the creek, so select 2½- to 3-foot boulders that are more round than angular, as creeks naturally round down and smooth stones. Try to match the purchased rocks to the native rocks on your property if you have them.

STEP 2: **Mark the creek bed:** Use the hose to create nice round curves, and then mark it out with marking spray. Mark out a path using both straight portions and sweeping curves to appear as natural as possible. (If the ground is very dry, mist it with a hose first for better adhesion.) I recommend defining a lawn or patio space with this shape, and it can even split off into two separate areas. The width should vary too, depending on how it curves and what elements the creek is working around. I made mine roughly 3 feet wide with a 2- to 5-foot variance as needed to appear natural and ended it with a washout of stones.

STEP 3: **Dig out the creek bed:** Using a spade shovel, dig out the center to roughly 18 inches. Pry out rocks with a breaker bar if needed. Taper your way back up to the natural grade as you reach the edge. You will have excess soil here, so use it to create mounding on the side or elsewhere in the yard. A flat bottom with 30- to 45-degree tapered or angled edges is best so that you can stack boulders and rocks.

**STEP 4:** **Anchor the boulders:** Your boulders define the layout, so pick the biggest and the best and place them in key spots along the edge. Transition areas or directional turns are great for accent boulders. Bury these boulders one-fourth to one-third into the side or the bottom of the creek bed, depending on where they sit.

**STEP 5:** **Roll out the landscape fabric:** Landscape fabric is used in most applications as a weed barrier and helps slow down erosion when water moves through it. Roll out the fabric and secure the material to the ground with landscape staples tapped in with a mallet. Make sure when you overlap pieces of fabric that they overlap by at least 3 inches. Cut the fabric with a utility knife as needed. Use large rocks from 6 to 12 inches on the flat edges to help hold the fabric and to outline your creek bed.

**STEP 6:** **Place the stones:** Stack some of the larger stones and place them around the boulders and other select areas as well as along the edges. Hand placing these rocks is the key; I've seen creek beds where the stones are just randomly scattered, and it looks messy and unnatural. The sides and top should be "fitted."

**STEP 7:** **Place the smaller stones:** Use a shovel to collect smaller rocks in a wheelbarrow and dump into place. The beige Mexican beach pebbles used here are the most expensive, well rounded and best-looking, so I saved them for the "top dressing." Make sure they cover all the visible landscape fabric. The more variety in stone sizes and the more deliberate the placement, the cleaner and more dynamic it will look. Place plants along the side of the creek bed to make it appear natural. Don't be surprised if you find sunbathing lizards and exploring kids enjoying this defining yard feature as much as you do!

# PEBBLE MOSAIC CARPET

**LEVEL: BEGINNER–INTERMEDIATE**
**COST: $$**
**TIME COMMITMENT: 2–3 DAYS (OR 1–2 WEEKENDS)**
**PROFESSIONALS NEEDED: NONE**
**DIMENSIONS: 2' × 4" × 8'**

Creating a mosaic carpet is a fun, creative project that adds a lot of character and personality to your yard. Instead of rolling out an outdoor rug, mark out an area for a permanent rug that will bring low-maintenance texture and art to the landscape. Each mosaic will be completely different depending on what stones are available and how you piece them together. Although it is not a complicated process, it is very time-consuming—but rewarding. This is a great project for people who like puzzles and are creative, and is a great conversation starter when you have friends and family over.

## TOOLS

- Gloves
- Tape measure
- Hand shovel
- Spade or flat/trenching shovel
- Wheelbarrow
- Hose and multispray nozzle
- Hand tamper
- Level
- Three to five 5-gallon buckets or containers to separate rocks if needed
- Trowel
- Scrap lumber
- Rubber mallet
- Sponge
- Paintbrush (optional, for applying muriatic acid if needed)

## MATERIALS

- Seven 50-lb bags of a variety of 2"–3" decorative stones, separated by size and color
- 1 can of marking spray
- Five 50-lb bags of ¾" base material
- Six 90-lb bags of type S mortar
- Scrap flagstone (optional)
- 1 gallon muriatic acid (optional, for cleaning off mortar)
- Wet sealer in application spray can

**STEP 1:** **Select your decorative stones:** This is the fun part! Pick out stones of contrasting colors and sizes. Flat round rocks are the best; Mexican beach pebble is a great choice. Similar size stones are best.

**STEP 2:** **Select your location and dig:** Using a tape measure and marking spray, measure and mark the dimensions of your space. If the ground is very dry, mist it with a hose first for better adhesion. Your location can be round, square or irregular, depending on your space. Symmetrical ovals, circles or squares will read more contemporary and modern while irregular will read more artsy or eclectic. This mosaic is defined by the flagstone patio surrounding it. Dig out an area that is 4 inches wider than the actual space and 4 to 6 inches deep. If you live in a climate that freezes, dig 4 to 8 inches deeper.

STEP 3: **Place the base and level it:** Using a shovel and wheelbarrow, backfill 2 to 3 inches with base material. Mist down the area with a hose and compact with a hand tamper. Use a level to create a slight 0.5 to 2 percent slope so surface water drains off.

STEP 4: **Mark the design:** Use the marking spray to generally define the areas of the carpet based on your design. I like to mark out the basic outline and then figure it out as I go. However, if you like more direction, find a pattern or inspiration online and use that as a reference. Keep it simple and graphic, as too much detail can get lost. For this project, I used three triangles as the main features and created detail inside and around them with bands and groupings of rocks of the same color and size.

STEP 5 **Sort your decorative stones:** It is important to sort your stones by color and size so you can work easily and quickly when you are ready to set your stone. You are looking for flat round stones between 1½ and 3½ inches. Place these in separate buckets.

**STEP 6:** **Mix a small batch of mortar:** Since this project can take a while, mix only as much mortar as you think you can use at a time; you can always mix more! You want a thick but workable consistency, so shoot for a smooth peanut-butter-like texture. With a trowel, add a layer 3 to 4 inches high and wide for the border of the triangle.

**STEP 7:** **Place your decorative stones:** To place the stone, inset them vertically into the mortar. In this project I started by piling up concrete in a diamond form. To prevent kicking out stones, cover two-thirds or more of the stone with mortar so that only the top one-third is revealed in the final design. You want your stones slightly higher than the grade around them so that water doesn't collect and stay. If you have scrap flagstone, incorporate it into your design to take up space and break up the pattern.

**STEP 8:** **Level and check:** Place your first stone and then use a 2 x 4 piece of lumber to verify that you're even with the surrounding grades. If a rock is too high, you can use a rubber mallet to tap it down. Mortar will press out on the sides, so let it stay until the stones are secure, and then clean up any excess with a trowel before finishing for the day; otherwise, it will be in the way of your next layer if you're not completing the project in a single day.

**STEP 9:** **Continue to set rocks:** I worked my way around one diamond, carefully selecting reddish rocks and stacking them as close as I could together. I let it sit for 10 to 15 minutes before taking a sponge with grout and working it between the joints. Continue on and keep creating patterns and motifs with different color and size rocks. The cleaner you are here, the better!

**STEP 10:** **Check the level:** Check your level as you go; remember, this is not going to be perfect because all the stones are different, but you can get close. You want to avoid big dips and peaks, as these create a tripping hazard.

**STEP 11:** **Sponge off the mortar:** Use a sponge to clean off the excess mortar residue. Keep it clean by rinsing it off every few swipes. You may need to return and clean again two or three times, because you don't want the mortar to dry on top of the stones.

**STEP 12:** **Clean up the residue:** If you didn't do a good job of cleaning off all the concrete residue on the rocks, wait until the surrounding mortar is set (24 hours or more). Mix up a solution of ½ pint of muriatic acid per gallon of water, apply it with a brush and scrub them down.

**STEP 13:** **Seal it:** I really want the pebbles to pop and contrast with the cement around them, so I used a wet sealer in an application spray can to cover the area.

**STEP 14:** **Finish it off:** Use small decorative stones that complement the colors of the design to fit in the areas surrounding the piece. You'll enjoy this mosaic as a conversation starter, as it adds detail and whimsy to your yard.

# CHAPTER 7

# LUMBER FOR EVERY PROJECT
## POPULAR EXTERIOR WOOD OPTIONS

Lumber is one of the most universal materials used in landscaping—everything from pergolas to benches can be made from lumber. But because lumber is an organic material, it's susceptible to its changing environmental surroundings, so it's important to consider the best material for the job. This chapter will explore the many varieties and grades of lumber, the pros and cons of each, and which lumbers are best suited for different applications. The projects will teach you how to make two stunning features that will dramatically enhance your outdoor space: a bench seat along a fence (page 102) and a screening wall (page 106) to bring privacy to your yard.

## OVERVIEW OF LUMBER

Lumber falls into two categories: hardwood and softwood. Hardwood and softwood are categorized by the tree's reproductive system. Angiosperms produce flowers and fruit, and gymnosperms typically produce cones or "naked seed" (which are neither flower nor fruit). Angiosperms include maple, oak, walnut and ipe, which are all hardwoods. Gymnosperms include redwood, cedar, Douglas fir and pine, and they are considered softwoods.

In general, softwoods are more affordable and easier to work with than hardwoods and globally are used significantly more often than hardwoods, which can be slower growing and denser than softwoods, making them more difficult and expensive to work with. Therefore, softwoods are used largely for building construction while hardwoods are usually reserved for fine finish work and furniture. Note that not *all* hardwoods are harder than softwoods and vice versa.

Most big box suppliers stock the basic types of lumber, such as Douglas fir, pressure-treated, plywood and cedar. Depending on your location, the selection may vary, but typically big box stores don't carry much more than high-use construction lumber. I prefer to go directly to a lumberyard, where the selection is greater and they usually stock a variety of woods at different grades, plus the staff are usually very knowledgeable.

## LUMBER GRADES

Lumber is graded in many different ways, depending on its intended use, aesthetics and quality. In a nutshell, one type of tree can produce a variety of qualities of lumber. Lumbers that are prettier, have few defects and are long-lasting grade higher and cost significantly more than, for example, knot-ridden, wide-grained lumber. But both lumbers are called by the same common name, such as redwood or cedar. There are so many choices within each category that it is wise to go to a yard to look at your options and chat about your individual project so you don't end up spending more than you need to. You don't always have to buy the highest-grade lumber. Sometimes a lower grade lumber can get you the same results and save you some money.

## SAPWOOD VS. HEARTWOOD

**Sapwood** is the live wood closest to the bark. This is what is responsible for the growth of the girth of a tree; when these cells die, they become part of the heartwood.

**Heartwood** is the lumber at the center of the tree that is already dead. Natural chemicals collect here that stain the wood darker and make it more resistant to fungus and insect infestation. This, plus the strength and beauty of heartwood, makes it the most desirable cut.

## EASE OF USE

Working with wood can be easy or difficult, depending on the type of wood you are building with, the tools you are using and your abilities. Some woods are easier to cut and manipulate than others, depending on the density, strength and grain structure of the wood. For example, ipe is a very dense hardwood and cutting through it will cause more wear and tear on your tools than cutting through cedar.

## CONSIDERATIONS

**LENGTH:** Determine the length of lumber you can fit in your car or truck before you buy it, or arrange for delivery.

**HEALTH:** Breathing sawdust is bad for your respiratory system and can cause allergy or sinus issues with overexposure. Wear a mask.

**SAFETY:** Always wear safety goggles, and keep loose clothes and hair tied back when cutting lumber.

**ACCURACY:** The classic rule is measure twice, cut once.

## COST

Lumber costs can vary greatly depending on the type of wood, the grade and where it is coming from as well as fluctuations in availability from region to region.

## MAINTENANCE

All wood will decompose over time, but some types will rot more slowly than others, and staying on top of maintenance is key to preserving your lumber as long as you can.

## PAINT OR STAIN

When you use lumber like cedar, redwood, ipe or teak, the grain is usually something you want to highlight. I stay away from painting these because they really shine best with a clear coat or a colored transparent or semi-transparent stain that enhances their color.

## USING LUMBER IN THE LANDSCAPE

Lumber availability can vary greatly from region to region. Following are some of the popular woods that can be found in most regions. All of these listed are suited for and used in exterior applications, from fences to decks to furniture. The availability of lumber can change with consumer popularity, current trends and natural influences, such as drought or fire. Lumber is one of the most versatile materials you can use in an exterior application and it can play just as easily into a modern theme as into a warm, rustic style. There are many options at a range of price points for various applications.

## DOUGLAS FIR: $–$$

**Native source:** North American West

**Description:** Relatively easy to work with and one of the strongest softwoods available, Douglas fir is used for everything from setting concrete forms to building pergolas and houses. It is widely available, which makes it a reliable source of lumber, but because it has minimal natural tannins to repel bugs, it is susceptible to critters and will rot if not protected and sealed. There are different grades of Douglas fir and some cuts are more reliable than others, but expect the standard lumber you get from a big box store to warp or twist as it adjusts to the elements and dries out.

**Pros:** Structurally strong, relatively affordable, widely available

**Cons:** Susceptible to insects, warping and twisting; is soft and indenting can occur with pencil pressure

### CEDAR, WESTERN RED CEDAR: $$

**Native source:** North American West

**Description:** There are a lot of different cedars available depending on where you live, but they all have somewhat similar qualities. Due to its natural odor and tannins, cedar produces chemicals, or "extractives," that protect the tree from rot and insect attacks. Cedar is one of my favorite lumbers for its versatility, ease of use, consistent coloring and beauty.

**Pros:** Longevity, naturally rot resistant and largely insect resistant, relatively affordable, beautiful

**Cons:** Soft and can dent

### REDWOOD: $$

**Native source:** California and Oregon

**Description:** Known for its rich color and resistance to pests and rot, redwood is a popular lumber choice. Old-growth redwood is hard to come by but is coveted when available. If you were to compare old-growth heartwood with new-growth sapwood, the differences would be very obvious. The young sapwood is like a watered-down version of old growth in terms of its desirable qualities. However, that doesn't mean there aren't great options still available without harvesting the remaining old-growth forest. Clear, all-heart redwood is the best, most insect- and rot-resistant, knot-free redwood you can get. Merchantable is the most affordable cut, with its imperfections, splits and knots.

**Pros:** Naturally repels insects and rot, relatively affordable, beautiful

**Cons:** Availability of old lumber is low, new growth is not as high quality; great variation in color from light white to red to brown, which can be a problem for some applications.

### PRESSURE-TREATED LUMBER: $$

**Native source:** Everywhere

**Description:** Pressure-treated wood is typically made from pine, and it is created by forcing a chemical compound into the exterior layers. The wood is rated differently depending on the amount and type of chemical used to preserve it; some are rated to withstand aboveground contact and others to withstand ground contact. The chemicals make the wood extremely resistant to fungus, bacteria and insects, which makes it a very valuable and long-lasting option to use outside. However, you should wear gloves when handling it and never use pressure-treated wood for vegetable beds. Also, use hot dipped galvanized or stainless steel screws, which are the most compatible with the chemicals in the wood.

**Pros:** Lasts a very long time, affordable, available, able to withstand ground contact

**Cons:** Lots of chemicals, not the prettiest of woods, cannot be used for certain applications (e.g., vegetable beds)

## EXTERIOR PLYWOOD: $

**Native source:** Everywhere

**Description:** Plywood is made by gluing thin pieces of wood veneer together with waterproof glue. It is affordable and easy to work with. Overall, plywood is a very strong material, but because of the possibility of separation over time due to moisture and fluctuations in temperature, I shy away from using it for high-end or long-lasting projects. This problem can be mitigated somewhat with waterproofing, stain and other weather-protecting upkeep.

**Pros:** Very affordable, easy to use, stable, strong

**Cons:** Standard looking, possibility of separating over time

## IPE (AKA BRAZILIAN WALNUT): $$$$

**Native source:** South and Central America

**Description:** Ipe is a tight-grained hardwood that is one of the densest and most difficult woods to work with, but it is admired for its strength and beauty. Ipe weathers extremely well and is naturally rot and insect repellent, which is why it is a popular choice for many homeowners. However, it is so dense that it slows down labor and dulls tools, so expect to replace or sharpen some blades after your project or to pay higher labor and material fees to your contractor. Since the material and labor costs are significantly higher than working with other woods such as redwood and cedar, ipe can blow a budget quickly, which is why it is not widely used.

**Pros:** Durable, beautiful, distinctive, long lasting

**Cons:** Expensive, difficult to glue, hard to work with, imported, dulls blades and tools

## TEAK (AKA BURMESE TEAK): $$$$

**Native source:** South Asia, but also Asia, tropical regions in Africa, and South and Central America

**Description:** Teak is a very popular hardwood and is admired for its consistent appearance. Because of its high oil content, teak is resistant to dry rot and termites. It is easy to work with, which makes it a very popular choice for furniture and exterior elements. However, teak sapwood is less resistant and durable than the heartwood, which contains the most natural oils, so expect differences in cost and performance over time.

**Pros:** Easy to work with, rot resistant, termite resistant, glues well

**Cons:** Expensive, imported

## COMPOSITE DECKING: $$$

**Native source:** Everywhere

**Description:** There are a lot of brands of composite lumber with different combinations of materials to create long-lasting, durable lumber replacements. These composite boards cost more initially but will save you on maintenance costs. Composite decking material is usually made from wood fibers, plastics and an adhesive or binder. Check with the manufacturer for joist requirements, as composite is not as rigid as wood and may require tighter or different supports. The average deck spacing for most decks is every 12 to 16 inches, while you can get away with 16 to 24 inches for some decks with real wood.

**Pros:** Long lasting, has a warranty, no maintenance

**Cons:** Expensive, requires more joists, requires specialty hardware

# FENCE BENCH

**LEVEL: BEGINNER TO INTERMEDIATE**
**COST: $$**
**TIME COMMITMENT: I AFTERNOON**
**PROFESSIONALS NEEDED: NONE**
**DIMENSIONS: 27½" W × 99" L × 27" H**

Adding seating to any yard is always a bonus, but tying it into an existing feature makes it that much more interesting and a better use of space. My buddy Maurice Temple and I came up with this idea when trying to squeeze some seating into a small area. It's simple, straightforward and pretty darn cute, if I do say so myself.

BEFORE

## TOOLS

- 6' level
- Drill and drill bits for pilot holes, countersink bit (optional)
- Tape measure
- Shovel
- Hand tamper
- Miter or circular saw
- 2' level
- Paintbrush (optional, if using stain)

## MATERIALS

- Six 2" × 6" × 10' boards
  - Two cut to 23½", for under bench support
  - Five cut to 88", for seat bench
  - Four cut to 27½", for armrest and side bench
- Four 2" × 4" × 10' boards
  - One cut to 99", for bench back support
  - Two cut to 23½", for under bench support
  - Four cut to 12", for vertical arm support
  - Twelve cut to 15", for decorative diamonds
  - Two cut to 26", for side arms
- One 4" × 4" × 8' board, cut to four 16" pieces (if sitting flush on ground) or cut to 22" (if set in concrete)
- One 1-lb box of 2½" exterior deck screws
- One 1-lb box of 2" exterior deck screws
- 8 GRK 2" lag screws
- 50-lb bag of ¾" gravel
- Stain (optional)
- Three 27½" wide × 33" long cushions (optional)

**STEP 1:** **Select your location:** Fences can be long and boring; select a space in your yard that could use a little breaking up and some added interest. I chose an area that is lightly shaded so it is comfortable most of the time and right next to the bocce ball court so that players can have an audience (or a rest). You don't need a lot of space, but make sure you have minimally 2 feet of walking distance in front of it. Most fences need a little modifying to support the extra weight of people sitting on the bench, so I removed all the boards and added a 2 × 4 support rail about 18 inches up from the ground. You can put the old fence boards back or replace them with new ones, which lets all the wood weather together.

**STEP 2:** **Mark the support stringer:** Using a 6-foot level, mark a straight line 18 inches up and 99 inches across. This is for the supporting stringer on the other side of the fence and gives you a reference as to where you will be attaching your lumber.

**STEP 3:** **Make the bench back:** Using the drill, secure with exterior screws the two 23½-inch 2 × 6s on the end of each side of your cut 99-inch 2 × 4s. Then measure 28 inches from the inside edge of your 2 × 6 and attach a 23½-inch 2 × 4 piece. Repeat on the other side so you have an inside open space measurement of 25½ inches.

**STEP 4:** **Attach the bench back:** Use the reference line that you marked in step 2 to attach your bench back. Secure with exterior screws and check your level.

**STEP 5:** **Add the posts:** Below where the posts will go, dig about 4 inches deep and 8 inches wide, fill with gravel and tamp down. Seat the 4 × 4 posts on the gravel and attach to the underside of the 2 × 4s and 2 × 6s with exterior screws. Two 4 × 4 posts will be placed lining up with the outside edge of the 2 × 6 top support on each side. The other 4 × 4s will be attached directly below the 2 × 4 supports placed in step 3.

**STEP 6:** **Attach the seat bench:** Take all five of the 88-inch 2 × 6-inch boards and line them up 1½ inches in on either side of the bench support. This will leave 4 inches exposed on either side.

**STEP 7:** **Attach the seat sides:** Take the 27½" 2 × 6 boards and secure them on the ends. They will overhang the 4 × 4 posts by 1½ inches, just enough to fit the 23½-inch 2 × 4 securely. Attach the 2 × 4 on each side to the 4 × 4 posts with exterior screws.

**STEP 8:** **Make the armrests:** Make one of your armrests by lining up two of the 12-inch 2 × 4s with the bottom of the horizontal 2 × 4. Measure 4 inches from the fence and attach one 2 × 4 with two 2-inch lag screws, then measure 4 inches from the front of the bench and attach with two 2-inch lag screws on the other 2 × 4 armrest support. Repeat on the other side. Cap off each vertical 2 × 4 with a 26" 2 × 6.

**STEP 9:** **Make the decorative diamonds:** These are super simple, and they finish off the bench and make it unique. With a miter saw, cut the edges on all twelve 15-inch 2 × 4s with a 45-degree angle so that they fit to make three perfect diamonds. Assemble the diamonds on the ground, securing 2-inch screws 1 inch up from each corner to secure the mitered edges at the outside corners. Use a level to mark out the locations of the diamonds. Find the center of the bench and measure up 12 inches; this is where the center diamond's bottom point will be. The diamonds are spaced 12 inches point to point on each side. Attach each corner of the assembled diamonds to the fence with 2-inch screws.

**STEP 10:** **Stain the wood, if desired:** Apply stain with a paintbrush or rag if desired, and let dry completely. I chose to leave the cedar raw so it could age and blend in with the cedar fence. Pop in your cushions, take a seat and enjoy the fruits of your hard work!

# PANEL SCREENING WALL

**LEVEL: BEGINNER TO INTERMEDIATE**
**TIME COMMITMENT: I DAY**
**COST: $$**
**PROFESSIONALS NEEDED: NONE**
**DIMENSIONS: 6" × 12'**

Privacy is one of the most common requests I hear from my clients, and building a panel wall is a wonderful solution—not only do you get the privacy, but you also get a beautiful backdrop that adds detail and style to your yard. Instead of having a standard fence, this filtered view will be a permanent statement piece that will enhance the mood of the space. Plus, it's easy to install once you get the support frame up!

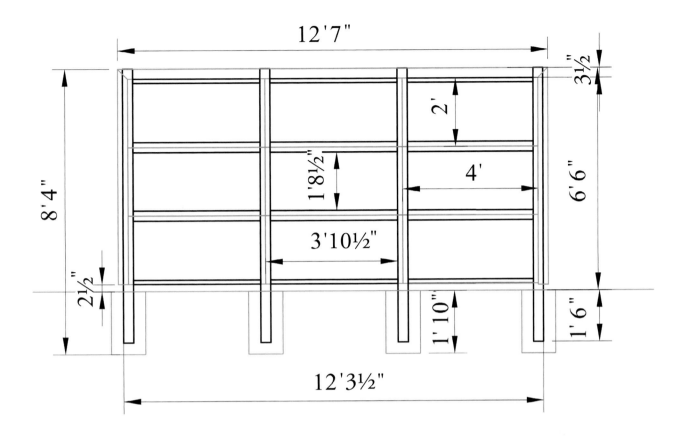

## TOOLS

- Shovel
- Measuring tape
- 5-gallon buckets or wheelbarrow
- 2' level
- Mason's string
- Drill with drill bits for pilot holes and countersink bit (optional)
- Finish nail gun (optional)
- Circular or miter saw
- Torpedo level (mini level)

## MATERIALS

- Twelve 50-lb bags of rapid-set concrete mix
- Four 4" × 4" × 10' pressure-treated posts
- Six 2" × 4" × 8' pressure-treated lumber, cut to twelve 44½" lengths
- One 1-lb box of 2½" exterior screws
- Nine 2' × 4' composite wood panels
- Two 2" × 4" × 8' cedar boards
- One 2" × 4" × 16' cedar board, cut to 12'7"

**STEP 1:** **Select your location:** You are probably well aware of areas in your yard that could use some privacy, but you might want to place this panel wall as a backdrop to an outdoor dining room or as a focal piece that you can see from inside the house. This feature could be added onto an existing fence or built freestanding, like this project.

**STEP 2:** **Set your posts:** Use a shovel to dig four holes that are 12 inches wide and 24 inches deep. Using a measuring tape, space them out so the posts sit 4 feet on center. Mix up two or three bags of concrete in 5-gallon buckets or a wheelbarrow to a thick but fluid constancy. Measure and mark 18 inches from the bottom of a 4 × 4 × 8 post, place in the center of the hole and pour concrete around it. Use a level to make sure each side is plumb. After the first post is set, use a mason's string to pull a straight line across to set the remaining three posts so that they are flush and in line with each other.

**STEP 3:** **Build the frame:** Measure 2 inches up from the bottom of the posts and attach a 44½-inch 2 × 4-inch board so the 2-inch side is facing you. Attach by toe nailing (screwing at a 45° angle, as shown in the photo) the piece to the 4 × 4 post on either side. Then measure 20½ inches up and set another 44½-inch 2 × 4-inch board, but this time set it wide so that the 4-inch face (wide side) is facing you. You will attach the 2-foot panels to these boards. The bottom runner will be covered and the top will be split between two panels, allowing the next layer to stack on top. Repeat this step across all posts and add another layer of 44½-inch 2 × 4s above and across. Measure up 20½ inches and run your 2 × 4's thin side (2-inch side) facing out to top off the frame.

**STEP 4:** **Predrill the panels:** Predrill all the screw attachments with a countersink bit or the screws will bulge out when you're done. Predrill in all four corners about ¾ inch in from both sides and in the center top and bottom of the panel about ⅔ inch up. You can also use a finish nail gun to attach these along the perimeter for a more seamless look.

**STEP 5:** **Attach the panels:** Line up and attach the first panel with the bottom 2 × 4 support post and halfway between the 4 × 4 posts on either side and make sure that it's level. Repeat to attack all nine panels.

**STEP 6:** **Build the decorative frame:** This is an optional step, but I feel that it really finishes off the project. With a circular or miter saw, cut the two 8-foot cedar 2 × 4s to 6 foot 4 inches with 45-degree mitered edges. Place them on the side 4 × 4 posts butting up to the edges of the end panels, covering the 2-inch revealed edge. Cut the top 16-foot board at a 45-degree angle on either side and attach the board with exterior deck screws across the top of the panels to create a frame. Now you have both privacy and a beautiful backdrop.

## CHAPTER 8

# COMMON METALS FOR EXTERIOR PROJECTS

## FROM BASIC ELEMENTS TO BEAUTIFUL BUILDS

Metal in the landscape can take many forms, such as functional chain link fencing, aluminum pergola structures and lighting fixtures. This chapter focuses on more creative uses of metal in the landscape to get you thinking of how you can incorporate and use it to enhance your yard. The project for a Decorative Patina Panel (page 114) is one such example, and I'll give you ideas and tips for others.

## OVERVIEW OF METAL

You can find basic metal, such as galvanized piping, corrugated metal and other common construction items, at big box stores. These can be used for their intended purpose or in creative ways. If you have access to a metal supply place, you'll have far more options and will probably get some interesting ideas, too.

### EASE OF USE

Depending on your project, it can be fairly easy to manipulate and assemble metal, or it can be complicated to weld, cut and create. Working with metal can be out of the realm of DIY for many people if you don't have the right tools or know-how. However, I don't let that stop me from designing and creating with it. I know very basic welding, but I rely on welders and fabricators to make projects for me, as they are skilled and know how to be safe when manipulating the material.

### CONSIDERATIONS

**SAFETY:** Metal is very sharp, especially when freshly cut, so be careful when handling it. Wear gloves and eye projection when cutting or manipulating.

**HEALTH:** Metal dust and shavings are dangerous to inhale; always wear a dust mask when working with it.

**TEMPERATURE:** Metal heats up quickly, whether in the sun or with a blade.

**PROTECTION:** Most metal needs to be protected from the elements to prevent rusting.

### COST

Metal is sold by weight or by piece/sheet, length or square footage. Depending on the type of metal, availability and quality, prices can vary a lot. In general, using metal in a landscape is an upgrade from, say, using composite or lumber for the same application, but not always.

### PROTECTION AND MAINTENANCE

Some metals, like corten steel and copper, do fine when exposed to the elements, but many metals, especially mild steel, need a protective layer to prevent rust and corrosion. Maintenance depends on the type of metal you are using and the desired effect. For example, you may want to let a piece of corten steel rust for aesthetic purposes. Raw steel is almost always powder-coated or painted to protect it from rusting, which requires touching up the protective paint. Copper, brass and bronze may be left to weather or patina. Quality stainless steel typically doesn't rust and is cleaned easily with vinegar and a paper towel from time to time. Overall, metal is fairly low maintenance.

**Powder coating** is the best protective layer option in my opinion because it is durable and long lasting and there are many color options. It is achieved by baking on a colored powder that is more durable than standard paints. It's not very DIY-friendly because it requires professional-level tools.

**Painting** is a bit more DIY-friendly. Protective metal paint can be applied with a sprayer or by hand and is widely available from any hardware store.

**Galvanization** is a protective zinc coat that is added to iron or steel to help prevent rusting. The most popular application is achieved by hot-dipping or submerging the metal piece in a vat of molten zinc. Galvanized steel has a characteristic speckled finish that represents the chemical reaction between the zinc and the steel created by hot-dipping.

## USING METAL IN THE LANDSCAPE

Metal is a popular item to use in the landscape, from benches to light fixtures to decorative details. I reclaimed old wrought iron gates from a client's house and made a decorative focal piece for the garden by securing them to a 4 × 4 frame (see page 150). Using metal can be purely decorative, as seen in the decorative panel project in this chapter; or structural, such as support beams for pergolas; or functional, as in corten steel planters. I love corten steel planters and retaining walls: the orange rust is so beautiful and can read as modern or rustic. Corten and mild steel sheets are great for decorative panels, whether solid with a patina or cut with a computer-controlled machine into a decorative design. You can literally design almost anything you'd like on paper and get a machine to cut it out exactly as you specify. Aluminum and corrugated steel make great covers and accent walls that can be left untreated or painted. Bands and bars of any kind of metal make great accents to a fence, wall or landscape decor.

The following are just a few types of metals that are popular and useful for functional and artistic features.

### STEEL: $–$$$

**Mild steel (aka carbon steel):** This is the most popular and available steel on the market by far. Mild steel is an alloy of iron and carbon. The carbon adds strength, but it also can make it brittle. Mild steel can contain only 0.25 percent carbon maximum and is valued for its ductile strength and affordability. Medium and high carbon steel never contain more that 2 percent carbon; although stronger and harder, they are also more brittle and less ductile.

**Corten steel:** This is a combination of steel alloys that has a protective layer to withstand rain, snow, fog and other moisture issues without a protective seal. If left to weather naturally, it will go from raw steel to a vibrant orange and then stabilize at a dark brown. I sometime seal the steel mid-rust to save the beautiful orange color as a permanent feature. Expect to pay at least twice as much for corten over standard mild steel.

**Corrugated steel panels:** These are universal and useful. The corrugated structure of the sheet increases its strength, so it can span long distances without sagging when used in a horizontal manner, such as for an affordable patio roof. It is typically used for siding and roofs, but you can create a modern industrial look by using it for fences or veneers on wood planters. Steel panels should have a protective seal to slow or prevent rusting.

**Stainless steel:** This metal must contain 11.5 percent chromium, which helps create a protective seal to withstand corrosion, rust and stains. There are many different grades available depending on the project needs.

## COPPER: $$$$

Copper is resistant to corrosion, easily manipulated and if left unfinished creates a beautiful patina. Whether used as a landscape accent or in an outdoor kitchen backsplash, copper is expensive but always beautiful. Copper alloyed with tin makes bronze, and copper alloyed with zinc makes brass.

## ALUMINUM: $$$

Aluminum is the most abundant metal element on earth, and second-most popular metal after steel. It is used for everything from foil to rooftops, and is lightweight and strong. It's available in a variety of alloys that range in strength and weldability depending on the application. Aluminum panels are also available and popular in areas near moisture or water, but are more easily dented.

## IRON: $$$

**Cast iron:** Cast iron is created by pouring molten iron into a mold. Because of the high carbon content (3 to 4 percent), it is very hard but also very brittle, which makes it nearly impossible to shape, thus limiting the possibilities. It is also prone to rust and must be treated with a protective coat if exposed to the elements. Although it is not as popularly used, cast iron gives a vintage look to gates and other details.

**Wrought iron:** This iron alloy is heated and then shaped with tools. Although it is not as "tough" as cast iron, it has better tensile strength, can be heated up and worked more easily and is less prone to rust (but it still needs a protective paint). Popular in the mid-nineteenth century, it is less common today because gates and railings and similar features can be made cheaper with steel. The Eiffel Tower is made out of wrought iron lattice.

# DECORATIVE PATINA PANEL

### LEVEL: BEGINNER
### COST: $
### TIME COMMITMENT: ½ DAY
### PROFESSIONALS NEEDED: NONE
### DIMENSIONS: 2'3" × 4'3"

Copper and copper alloys such as bronze and brass have a blue-green patina that is very appealing, but they can be quite expensive metals to work with, especially for an art piece in which there is potential for error. Other metals, such as steel, are much more affordable but need to be prepared properly with a bronze or copper base or painted/stained to get the same effect, and then must be sealed so they don't rust. As with any metal project, be sure to wear protective gear and finish the piece with a clear protective seal or it will rust.

BEFORE

## TOOLS

- Gloves (handle all metal with gloves as edges are very sharp and can cut you)
- Clean rag
- Chip paintbrush
- Miter saw
- Drill and drill bit
- Stud finder
- Wire cutters

## MATERIALS

### PANEL

- 2' × 4' 24-gauge steel panel
- Household cleaner (such as Simple Green)
- Metal effects patina activator, base and bronze paint kit (to cover 30 sq ft)

- One 10-oz bottle of blue-green oxidized dye
- 1 roll of high-quality painter's tape (such as FrogTape)
- 1 can of teal spray paint
- 1 can of clear matte sealer

### FRAME

- Two 2" × 6" × 8' boards, cut to the following dimensions:
  - Two cut with mitered edges to 4'9"
  - Two cut with mitered edges to 2'9"
- 1" × 6" × 6' cedar fence board
- One 1-lb box of 1½" galvanized screws
- One 1-lb box of ¼" self-piercing pan-head screws
- Two 3" stucco screws
- Two ½" washers (to go with the 3" stucco screws)
- Two ½" eye hooks
- One 10' roll of 20-gauge wire (to hang frame; double it up if needed)

## PANEL

STEP 1: **Select the project location:** This panel, or "art" board, can be incorporated into any wall or structure in any size. For this project, I chose a blank wall, as it needed some visual interest.

STEP 2: **Clean the metal:** Your steel panel will have a thin film of grease that protects it from rusting, so you will need to remove this to be able to access the surface of the material. Use any standard household cleaner like Simple Green or soap and water with a clean rag. Spray and wipe it off.

STEP 3: **Prepare the base:** Apply the metal paint primer included in the patina kit with the chip brush. This protects the steel from the activator, which will be applied after two coats of primer and two coats of the bronze paint. Use a brush to cover the area entirely, wait 30 minutes, and then apply a second layer of primer. Let set overnight to dry properly.

STEP 4: **Use tape to make a design:** Now that your board has some layer of finish, use a high-quality painter's tape to create patterns or designs on the panel. Apply some pressure to the tape so that all of the edges are sealed thoroughly. I think abstract shapes in repetition are a good choice for this project because the patina is somewhat abstract and unpredictable, so you will lose a lot of detail.

STEP 5: **Apply the reactive paint:** Apply a consistent layer of the bronze reactive paint from the patina kit. Let the coat dry for 30 minutes.

**STEP 6:** **Apply the activator:** Apply one more coat of reactive paint and then apply the activator while the paint is still wet. I strategically sprayed the activator heavily in certain areas. The activator gives you a patina in a matter of minutes rather than months or years, which is the natural course. Because you are applying it, you can control the overall look and depth of the patina and lock it in place with a sealer to prevent oxidation, which causes the color change.

**STEP 7:** **Rotate the panel while wet:** You will have a little bit of playtime to adjust where the activator goes. I heavily sprayed the top portion of the panel, and then tilted the panel so the activator would run down and make a dripping effect. You can tilt it back and forth depending on your desired effect.

**STEP 8:** **Add more paint (optional) and remove the tape:** Use the teal spray paint and oxidized dye to touch up areas around the tape that the patina didn't hit and to add variation. After it is dry to the touch, peel away the painter's tape to reveal the pattern underneath.

**STEP 9:** **Seal the panel:** Use a matte sealer and apply liberally to cover every inch of the panel, including the sides and the back. Any exposed steel will rust.

## FRAME

STEP 1: **Build the frame:** Build a custom wooden frame out of 2 × 6s to house the piece of metal because the edges are sharp and you don't want to leave them exposed. Plus, the frame makes it look like a finished piece. Cut all your pieces to the cut list above and assemble on the ground.

STEP 2: **Make and attach the mending plates:** Using a scrap fence board, cut 5½-inch triangles with a miter saw to make mending plates. This is how you will attach your 2 × 6s together. Predrill six holes, three on each side, and then use 1½-inch screws to attach the mending plates to the cedar 2 × 6s.

**STEP 3:** **Attach the eye hooks and wire:** Attach two eye hooks to the back of the wood frame about 1½ inches down from the top. Cut 60 inches of the 20-gauge wire, fold it over on itself and twist it together to make a thicker and stronger wire. Tie to each end of the eye hooks.

**STEP 4:** **Place the stucco screws:** Using a stud finder, find two studs; most are spaced about 16 inches apart. Predrill holes in the studs and then attach the two stucco screws and two washers to anchor them into the wall. The screws should be spaced about 16 inches apart.

**STEP 5:** **Attach the panel to the frame:** The metal sheet should sit at about a 1-inch inset on all sides of the wooden frame. Using self-piercing pan-head screws and a drill, attach the panel with screws at least every 12 inches.

Hang the frame on the stucco screws. Now you have a custom art piece that can withstand the elements and elevates the aesthetic value of your yard. Outdoor art will be a conversation starter for sure!

# CHAPTER 9

# MASONRY AND CONCRETE DESIGN OPTIONS

## BUILDING A YARD THAT WILL LAST

One of the most versatile and useful materials out there is concrete. In fact, concrete is the most widely used construction material in the world, used twice as much as timber and steel and second only to water as a material used in construction. Most modern concretes use Portland cement as the standard binder; different admixtures are used to create products with various properties. Concrete can read modern, industrial or rustic, depending on how it is incorporated or applied. There are many uses for concrete in the landscape, from purely functional to aesthetic applications, including pools, poured-in-place patios, footings and post holes, and pots or other decorative items. Because concrete is such a versatile material, the opportunities are endless. This chapter will cover how to use concrete; color and finish options; the forms it can take, such as blocks, bricks and pavers; and the mortars and grouts used to set and finish concrete structures. The project in this chapter will show you how to build an affordable recycled retaining wall with plant cutouts (page 126).

## OVERVIEW OF CONCRETE

Concrete has compressive strength (ability to withstand compression) that can vary depending on the mix of materials; a range from 2,500 to 4,000 pounds per square inch (PSI) is standard for most residential landscape applications. However, the tensile strength (ability to withstand tension) of concrete is weak, so reinforcing bar, or "rebar," is used to reduce cracking and hold the concrete together. A lot of people say "cement" when they really mean concrete. Cement is just a binder, and concrete is the mixture of cement, sand, aggregate and water.

### EASE OF USE

You can buy premixed bags of concrete with different strengths and uses from a hardware store or big box store. Concrete is usually sold in 50-, 60-, 80- or 94-pound bags. It is more cost-effective to buy the large bags, but if they are too heavy for you to lift, consider buying the 50-pound bags to save your back. Sometimes I split a bag right down the center and take half a bag at a time . . . on the job site . . . not at the store!

For large concrete projects that are not poured all at once from a truck, such as a mortared block wall, it is most affordable to mix your own concrete. I use C-mix, which is a combination of pea gravel and sand, and mix that with Portland cement. Half a 94-pound bag of Portland cement to 24 to 26 standard shovelfuls of C-mix is a good standard mix. Post holes do better with larger aggregate, so I add ¾-inch gravel to the mix if I am using C-mix for setting posts. C-mix is usually ordered by the ton or the yard and delivered in large bags, or dumped in your driveway or at your curb.

Ordering a concrete truck is the most efficient way to cover a large area. If you are pouring a patio or a large space, you definitely want to order a truck, which can hold up to 10 yards of concrete. If you don't need that much, you can order a partial load or short load, but they actually charge you more for that! You will also have to hire a pump and finishers, because concrete needs to be actively worked as it is poured. I don't recommend finishing concrete yourself—it's a special skill that you don't want to "learn" on your new patio . . . it is a pretty expensive mistake because you only get one try.

### MAINTENANCE

For the most part, masonry is very low maintenance, if installed correctly. Painting or spraying a protective sealer over concrete, pavers and even flagstone can help reduce stains, which can be helpful in areas near food and drink. Sometime sealers are also used to enhance the look of the product; a "wet" sealer will darken or provide gloss to the surface of pavers, concrete and flagstone, making it look like you just hosed it down.

### COLORS

Concrete doesn't have to be boring gray! There are several ways to add color to it.

**Integral color.** Integral means a liquid or powdered color is added to concrete while it is being mixed. It is a fairly affordable add-on that brings a nice depth to the material, but it can get quite expensive for certain colors, including blues, greens and black.

Most of my clients like the low to mid-range price point colors anyway, since those neutral tones tie in best with the natural environment.

**Stain.** Acid-based stains and water-based stains are applied to concrete after it has set. Acid-based stains chemically react with the hardened powder or "cream" of the concrete to change the color. If all you have is exposed aggregate on the top of your concrete, there is less material to absorb the stain. Acid stains can be toxic to work with, so be prepared with all the protective gear. Water-based stains penetrate the surface of concrete, giving a more consistent look because no chemical reaction is occurring. With any stain, if your concrete chips, you will see the lighter natural color below. Note that all colored stains bring out imperfections in the concrete, so if your concrete is dirty with grease stains, it will highlight them. This could work for some rustic or industrial looks . . . or just look bad.

**Concrete paint.** Paint can be applied to any concrete surface that is clean. This is a topical treatment that sits on top of the concrete, so it does have the potential to get scratched or peel off, although some brands provide better adhesion than others.

## FINISHES

A variety of finishes can be applied to concrete while it is still wet. Here are a few popular ones.

**Broom finish.** This is the standard finish, as it is the most affordable. A broom is brushed over mostly set concrete to create grooves that keep the concrete from being slick. I usually call for a light broom finish, just to have a little texture but not have overly obvious grooves.

**Top cast finish.** This is an add-on finish that etches the top of the concrete, revealing the aggregate below. There are different levels of etching, from a light, acid wash look to full aggregate exposure, depending on the aesthetic you're trying to achieve.

**Rock salt finish.** Large salt crystals are sprinkled on top of setting concrete, pressed in with a roller and later washed away, leaving decorative voids.

**Float or trowel finish.** Patterns can be made with a trowel or float as the concrete is setting up. I don't recommend this as a DIY finish unless you have a steady hand and trust your eye to keep your decorative stokes uniform.

**Stamped finish.** A stamped finish provides texture and can mimic the look of other materials, such as brick or flagstone (see the photo on page 123).

**Concrete overlay.** This is achieved when a thin layer of concrete is applied over an already installed concrete pad, and it is often decoratively stamped, stenciled or colored for a more interesting look. Although there is great technology for this, you run the possibility of this thin surface chipping off over time with wear and tear.

**Sealant.** Concrete can be left bare or sealed, as a matter of preference. A matte sealer is commonly applied as a protective layer against stains. A glossy seal will also protect from stains and give you a wet concrete look that will be darker than the existing color.

## TERMINOLOGY

Like any field, concrete construction has its own terminology, and it is important to understand what each term means so you can communicate with your contractor or follow a DIY project.

**Admixture:** An admixture is a material added to a concrete or cement mix to alter or enhance certain properties, such as speeding up hydration, slowing down setting time or making the mix stronger.

**Cement:** Cement is not concrete; it is the binding element that holds together the other materials that make up concrete.

**Concrete:** Concrete is the combination of water, sand, aggregates (rocks) and cement and sometimes other admixtures to manipulate the curing time, workability or strength.

**Hydration:** Mixing cement with water forms a chemical compound that binds the materials together and solidifies the mass.

**Mortar:** This mixture of sand and cement paste adheres stones, blocks or bricks together.

**Set or setting:** When liquid or malleable cement hardens to a solid, it "sets." Most standard concrete mixes fully set in about 28 days.

## USING MASONRY IN THE LANDSCAPE

Prefabricated concrete in the form of blocks, bricks and pavers serve many uses: CMU blocks are a common choice for retaining walls, bricks can be used to make planter walls and pavers can be laid for pathways. All can be used interchangeably for many different landscape projects. For example, a brick path and a paver path are installed in a very similar manner; a block wall and a stacked paver wall also use similar techniques. Many people prefer the look of pavers and bricks to the look of cement slabs, as they tend to be a little more interesting and inherently have more texture and color. Prefabricated concrete blocks and pavers are usually made out of a concrete material while bricks are typically made from clay.

Most of these prefabricated materials can be purchased at landscape yards, construction suppliers or big box stores. On average, installing pavers or bricks is more labor-intensive than pouring concrete, but get a quote for your particular project so you can make an educated decision.

### BRICKS: $–$$

A tried-and-true classic, bricks have been around for thousands of years. They are made out of sun-dried or fired clay and usually used in pathways, patios or vertically on walls and buildings. There are thousands of types of bricks in a wide range of colors, sizes, shapes and intended uses.

### CONCRETE PAVERS: $$–$$$

Pavers are made in all different shapes, sizes, strengths and colors. They are very popular for pathways, patios, driveways and other flat surfaces. Interlocking pavers are the most widely used, as they are extremely durable. They are a more affordable option than stone and the installation is similar to that of brick, which is labor-intensive.

### CONCRETE BLOCKS: $–$$

Concrete blocks, or concrete masonry units (CMUs), are basic building blocks made out of concrete. They are commonly used to build structures like outdoor counters, fireplaces, retaining walls, seat walls and other vertical features. CMUs are typically placed on a concrete footing, reinforced with rebar and mortared together for a very strong and reliable structure. The blocks can be left bare or finished with stucco or some sort of stone, tile or architectural concrete veneer.

### NURSERY BLOCKS: $–$$$

Nursery blocks are decorative, stackable concrete blocks used for small retaining walls, seat walls and planters. They come in different sizes and colors. Most interlock, and some just stack; most require a compacted base rather than a concrete footing.

## URBANITE: FREE–$

A scrap material created from broken concrete, urbanite can be used in many ways, from borders to retaining walls. Ideal pieces are 12 to 18 inches wide and 3 to 4 inches thick; any larger and they are hard to move around, and any smaller and they look like rubble. Urbanite is not typically sold in stores but can be easily found through demolition contractors, who are happy to get rid of it to avoid dump fees. Concrete with mesh or lots of rebar makes poor urbanite, as it crumbles and breaks when demolished.

## MORTARS AND GROUT

Although mortars are generally seen as different from concrete, they are very similar in nature. Mortars are a mixture of water, cement, sand, lime and sometimes other admixtures to alter the characteristics. They are used to bind prefabricated or natural units like bricks, blocks and stones and are typically mixed thicker than concrete. Don't substitute mortar and concrete for each other, as they have distinct intended uses. Below are the common types of mortars.

**Type S.** This is a mixture of 2 parts Portland cement, 1 part lime and 9 parts sand and is a strong mortar at 1,800 PSI. It is good for in-ground and above-ground applications and is stickier and sets faster than other mortars, making it a nice choice for vertical veneers such as architectural stone.

**Type N.** This is a mixture of 1 part Portland cement, 1 part lime and 6 parts sand. It is a medium-strength mortar, but is good for extreme weather or high heat, such as a fireplace. It has nice workability and is good for above-ground walls.

**Type M:** This is a mixture of 3 parts Portland cement, 1 part lime and 12 parts sand. It has very high compression strength because it has the biggest proportion of cement. It's typically used for above- and below-grade load-bearing walls.

**Grout.** Grout is a thin, mortar-like material that is used to fill in between tiles, stones or other masonry joints. Sometimes a regular mortar is used instead, such as for filling the joints of wet-set flagstone. Sanded grout is used for joint spaces between ⅛ and ½ inch, and non-sanded grout is used for spaces ⅛ inch or less. I prefer the look of the sanded grout. Grout comes in a variety of colors and should be thought of as part of the design aesthetic.

# URBANITE RETAINING WALL

**LEVEL: INTERMEDIATE**
**COST: $**
**TIME COMMITMENT: 1–2 WEEKENDS**
**PROFESSIONALS NEEDED: NONE**
**DIMENSIONS: 14" × 90'**

Urbanite is simply broken or repurposed concrete, and in this project it is used to create a unique and affordable retaining wall. By recycling the material out of your own yard or sourcing it from someone else's, you can usually get urbanite for free, saving you hundreds to thousands of dollars. Urbanite can fit into many styles, from a deconstructed modern look to rustic and reclaimed, depending on how it's organized. Adding plants can soften and green up the look and will add a little maintenance in terms of watering.

## TOOLS

- Gloves
- Measuring tape
- Wheelbarrow
- Transfer or flat-head shovel
- Spade shovel
- Digging bar for tough soils
- Hand tamper
- 5-gallon buckets or wheelbarrow
- Level

## MATERIALS

- 120–150 sq ft of urbanite (broken concrete) at least 12" wide and about 4" thick
- 3.25 yards or 150 (80-lb) bags of concrete (footing) or 3.25 cubic yards of gravel (for a 90-linear-ft wall)
- 1 cubic yard gravel for backfill
- Fifty to sixty 94-lb bags of type S mortar
- Landscape fabric
- One 1.75-cubic-yard bag of planting soil
- Four or five succulents or cascading plants (consider *Crassula* 'Campfire', *Dichondra* 'Silver Falls', *Sedum morganianum*, *Senecio rowleyanus* and *Tradescantia pallida* 'Purple Heart')

**STEP 1:** **Find your material:** Since urbanite, or broken concrete, is not readily available at stores, you need to search online neighborhood platforms, contact demo crews or call your local dump to see if you can source materials from there. Most people are happy to get rid of it, but make sure that you are not getting a pile of rubble. You want at least 12-inch pieces.

**STEP 2:** **Locate your project:** Select an area that needs retaining or create your own level by building up vertically. If you're working on a slope, cut it back so you have a flat area. You'll want to keep the height of your wall under 3 feet or at the height dictated by local code.

**STEP 3:** **Create the base:** Since this is a low wall, a compacted base of gravel or a concrete footing is fine. A concrete footing is a little more stable in general. Measure and dig 6 to 8 inches deep and 12 to 20 inches wide, depending on how big your urbanite pieces are and how high you are building. Mix the concrete in a wheelbarrow and pour a concrete footing and level it as you go, or fill it with base gravel and compact it with a tamper. Your project dimensions will probably vary from this description; a good calculator to figure out how much concrete you might need is available at www.concretenetwork.com/concrete/howmuch/calculator.htm.

**TIP:** *Instead of ordering bags of concrete, save money by mixing your own. Buy sand and gravel in bulk, or premixed (sold as C-mix) and mix with Portland cement at a ratio of 1 part cement, 2 parts sand and 3 parts gravel, or in other words, 1 shovelful of cement for every 5 shovelfuls of C-mix. Half a 94-pound bag of Portland cement to 24 to 26 standard shovelfuls of C-mix is a good ratio.*

**STEP 4:** **Build the first layer:** The first layer of the wall should sit right on top of your gravel or concrete base. The urbanite can be dry set, meaning stacked on top of each other with no mortar, or wet set with mortar. I find wet set is easier to level as you stack the layers because you can build up the low areas as needed, especially if you're using smaller pieces. Mix up the mortar in a 5-gallon bucket or wheelbarrow, if using.

Start on one corner and work your way across the bottom layer, leveling as you need to. We placed the urbanite pieces directly in the partially set-up concrete. You can also pour your footing and come back later and mortar on the first layer of urbanite. Leave pockets or holes for drainage on the bottom and throughout the wall here and there to alleviate water pressure buildup that can make a wall fail.

**STEP 5:** **Continue the layers:** Continue to set and level the urbanite pieces, staggering the seams (set the urbanite between the seams of the row below instead of lining the joints up).

**STEP 6:** **Manage the mortar:** Clean up any excessive mortar while it is wet because it will be hard to manipulate later. Because this wall is "reclaimed," you can get away with it being messy. If you want a more contemporary or tailored look, then be tidy and clean.

**STEP 7:** **Leave voids:** Leave random-sized voids in the wall for drainage but also so that you can plant succulents or other cascading plants later on. Make sure the void reaches all the way to the open space in the back. Finish the last layers of the wall.

**STEP 8:** **Backfill the wall:** Fill the back of the wall with ¾-inch gravel or any sort of aggregate to improve drainage. Separate the backfill from the dirt with landscape fabric and then backfill with soil.

**STEP 9:** **Tamp down:** Use a hand tamper to compact the newly placed soil to help prevent settling or sinking in the future.

**STEP 10:** **Make planting pockets:** Fill some of the large voids in the retaining wall with planting soil where you want to place plants.

**STEP 11:** **Plant:** Select a succulent or cascading plant that can thrive on little water or attention. Since this wall is south facing, it gets pretty hot, especially since it is surrounded by concrete, so this *Crassula* 'Campfire' succulent is a great choice. In fact, it actually turns redder the more sun it gets, making a nice contrast to the light-colored concrete. Not much maintenance is required, but be sure to hand water the succulents every few days until they are established or grown into the soil behind the wall; then you can cut back to watering once a week or as needed. You'll enjoy all the extra space gained by your new retaining wall and the cascading succulents for years to come!

# GETTING MOTHER NATURE ON YOUR SIDE

## PLANTS, SOIL AND GARDEN-ENHANCING FEATURES FOR YOUR BEST YARD YET

The living aspect of your yard is what makes your landscape a garden, an oasis, a home. Understanding what you want out of your yard and what your yard needs from you to thrive is a balance that you will discover over time. Spending time outside tending to your yard is good for you and your garden.

## THE LIVING PART OF YOUR YARD

For most people, the living landscape is often the most challenging element of the yard because it is ever changing. Unlike a hardscape patio that you can count on to be the same season to season, you can expect your trees, shrubs and other plants to change with the seasons and the weather. This constant change is welcomed by some and dreaded by those who aren't interested in keeping up with a landscape's shifting needs. Understanding the basics of living elements like soil and plants is the key to keeping your landscape healthy and happy.

Your landscape is part of a bigger ecosystem. Even a manicured non-native landscape still provides food and shelter for critters, insects, bacteria and fungi. All of these living elements coexist, and your actions can either enhance or disturb the ecosystem. The ecosystem, in turn, will work with or against your efforts. In theory, most people like the idea of a sustainable garden, but in practice many decide to smother everything in concrete instead, which is never a good idea.

## LANDSCAPE AND PROPERTY VALUE

Plants add a lot of value beyond the monetary kind; they make a big impact on your overall aesthetics and are responsible for setting the mood and style of a place. A wild, unkempt yard will reflect poorly on a home's upkeep, whereas a well-maintained space can make even the humblest abode sing. Big trees, especially in the front yard, can bring energy savings. If you have a big tree in your yard and you want to put a monetary value on it, check out www.treebenefits. com/calculator.com. Smaller plants and shrubs in general don't increase property value, but they create an overall impression that reflects well on the home. Increasing your curb appeal can do a lot for a first impression, which is why it is a worthwhile endeavor, as it is easy and affordable. Plus, there are plenty of professionals to help you out if you don't have the time.

Still, every aspect of your living landscape requires some knowledge of what will thrive in your location and what will work in a particular ecosystem, and the choices can seem overwhelming. This section will help you navigate the basic aspects of your yard—including plants, soil, gardens, lawns and options for built garden features—so that you can make the best choices for your home, lifestyle and environment.

# CHAPTER 10

# UNDERSTANDING PLANTS AND SOIL

## STARTING FROM THE BOTTOM UP

Soil is often overlooked as merely the filler or base for your projects and plants. Without digging deeper—literally and figuratively—most people don't consider it any further. But soils can vary widely in structure, texture and content, which will greatly influence your garden and overall landscape. This chapter will teach you about the components of soil and how to improve the soil in your yard to support healthy plants. A project for a Worm Composting Bin (page 135) is a fun, teachable tool for the family that will provide a steady supply of excellent nutrients for your garden.

## SOIL: STARTING FROM THE GROUND UP

Soil is not "dirt." Soil is alive; it is teaming with critters like worms, nematodes, bacteria and fungi that all work together, balancing each other out in a complex and complete system. In the same way that your gut has a balance of bacteria that keeps you healthy, soil also has its own ecology, and when things get out of whack, so does the overall health of the system. Chemical fertilizers can kill or compromise this system, creating the need for the continuous use of fertilizer to feed the plants because the soil's ability to supply nutrients has been damaged.

Like soil, dirt is composed of sand, silt, clay and other minerals, but it is largely sterile, or lacking most of the beneficial organisms that soil has. All dirt has the potential to be soil and usually already contains all the minerals a plant needs, but those nutrients are not available to plants in the correct form or proportions. Amending it with organic matter and compost introduces vital elements that will allow the nutrients and minerals already in the dirt to become available to your plants.

## OVERVIEW OF SOIL

Soils can range greatly from region to region and even neighborhood to neighborhood. Although not extremely common in residential practice, soil samples are usually taken on big jobs with lots of plants to determine the composition of nutrients and soil texture. This information is used to either revise the plant selection to match the soil type or to amend the soil to support the plant selection. Of course, it is easier to pick your plants based on your soil, but amending soil is something that you should probably do anyway.

Soil texture is determined by the combination of sand, silt and clay in a sample. The ideal soil for most gardens is loam, which has enough sand for good drainage and enough clay and silt for better water and nutrient retention.

**Sand** creates large pores in the soil that encourage good drainage and air space, but too much sand can lead to excess drainage and not enough water retention.

**Silt** is a mid-sized mineral that helps retain water and nutrients. Wet silt feels like silk when rolled between your fingers; dry silt is fine like powered sugar.

**Clay** is the finest particle, creating the fewest air pockets and the most water and nutrient retention. A heavy clay soil will swell and shrink with moisture and drought, which can be a problem for some structures.

The Natural Resources Conservation Service (NRCS) has a great online platform and database for information about the soil in your area. Start your own web soil survey by checking out http://websoilsurvey.sc.egov.usda.gov/App/HomePage.htm. Or take a sample from your own yard and mail it to a testing site, such as your county's Cooperative Extension Service, for results and recommendations.

## USING SOIL IN THE LANDSCAPE

It's not enough to just bring in a load of loam and dump it in your yard. You first need to understand several factors that affect soil composition and utility, including your climate, whether you use organic or nonorganic products, the extent of mycorrhizal fungi in the soil and whether you plan to use native or non-native plants in your yard.

**Climate.** It's important to understand your climate so you can work with it, not against it. Many urban-modern landscapes have little reference to their natural environment, meaning they are based on "ideals" that don't necessarily make sense in your area, such as a tropical garden in a desert. Such gardens will require a lot of maintenance to remain healthy and look great. Ask yourself what you are trying to achieve. Ultimately, you can have whatever kind of garden you'd like, but working with nature is a lot easier and makes more sense ecologically than importing a garden from another region. You can get clues to successful plantings by observing what is growing well around your part of town.

**Organic versus nonorganic.** Typically, people want to keep their edible gardens organic but are indifferent to the rest of the landscape. Whenever I can, I choose the organic route: it is safe, effective and natural, and supporting nature's systems is better for the overall environment. Purchase organic soils, fertilizers and other garden products. Always use organic products on vegetable beds, and never use pressure-treated wood to build edible garden beds.

**Mycorrhizal fungi.** Mycorrhizal fungi form a symbiotic relationship with plant roots. Almost all the terrestrial plants in the world are receptive to this fungus, as it has an extreme ability to gather nutrients and water available in the soil, extending the plant's reach by a significant amount. Mycorrhizal fungi feed off carbon from the plant in exchange for the nutrients and water. This support system creates a healthier and hardier plant that can better withstand drought and other stressors. Healthy soils have mycorrhizal fungi, but sterile or isolated soils often lack this vital system because there is not enough plant material to feed it. You can buy mycorrhizal fungi in a few different forms from nurseries and garden stores. This is key to a successful natural garden.

**Native versus non-native plants.** While an all-native garden is ideal for any environment, many people are not conditioned to appreciate them because our landscapes are so far removed from what they used to be. Growing native plants is very beneficial to the local wildlife, which have evolved to rely on these plant communities. Depending on what your style and architecture call for, it may make sense to stray from a native landscape, but always choose plants that can handle your climate. I choose to design to the style of the home and the local environment. I prefer to create hybrid gardens of native and/or climate-friendly non-native plants, depending on the client and the home.

If you have the opportunity and desire to go for natives, you'll be surprised how comfortable they make your space, because they are meant to grow in your area. However, many natives do look best with some "gardener's intervention," such as compost fertilizers, trimming and irrigation, to make them feel like a garden rather than an open space. A little grooming helps natives look more like a garden and less like an untended patch.

# WORM COMPOSTING BIN

### LEVEL: BEGINNER
### COST: $
### TIME COMMITMENT: AFTERNOON OR LESS
### PROFESSIONALS NEEDED: NONE
### DIMENSIONS: 30" × 20"

Compost, especially worm compost, is one of the most nutrient-rich composts available. It can take soil from futile to fertile and quickly give your whole yard a boost in growth and overall health. Think of worm compost as a superfood for your plants and soil. It is an easy and effective way to recycle food scraps and nourish your plants, plus it can be a great project and learning experience for the whole family.

## TOOLS

- Gloves
- Garden hose or water
- Drill and ¹⁄₁₆" drill bit

## MATERIALS

- Two 10-gallon stacking containers
- 1 coconut coir fiber block
- Handful or more of redworms (you can buy these online or at some nurseries)
- 2 shovelfuls of brown leaf litter and/or shredded paper
- 1 shovelful of greens (vegetable trimmings, lawn clippings, etc.)

STEP 1: **Select your containers and location:** You can use any double stacking containers that leave minimally 1 inch of space on the bottom when stacked. A 10- to 20-gallon container is a good size. Place your container in a shady area with indirect light, as the sun will make it too hot for the little critters, plus the compost will create its own heat as it decomposes.

STEP 2: **Soak the coconut coir fiber:** Place the coconut coir fiber block inside one of the containers. Fill the container with enough water to submerge the block. Let stand for 15 to 20 minutes, until it expands to double its size. If you have a large container you will have to pour out some of the excess water after it expands, or use a smaller bucket to soak the block and then transfer it to the large container.

STEP 3: **Fluff it out:** Use your hands to fluff out the coconut coir fiber to fill the bottom of the container. It should be about as wet as a damp sponge.

STEP 4: **Drill air holes:** With a drill and $\frac{1}{16}$-inch drill bit, drill holes around the top and bottom of the other container every 1 to 2 inches.

STEP 5: **Transfer the coconut coir:** Transfer the coconut coir fiber to the container with holes.

STEP 6: **Add the worms:** Add the worms to the container with the coconut coir fiber.

STEP 7: **Layer:** Cover the worms with a layer of brown leaves, a layer of the greens and then another layer of brown leaves.

STEP 8: **Stack the containers and feed the worms:** Stack the container with the worms on top of the solid container and place the lid on it. Feed the worms dried leaves, lawn cuttings and fruit and vegetable scraps once or twice a week. Till it into the top of the soil so it easier to access and will decompose better. My worms love the leftover fiber from my juicer. If you feed them large chunks of vegetables it could take a long time for them to decompose and they might start rotting, so chop them up! Never ever feed the worms any meat, oil or feces of any kind, as it will bring in bacteria that will smell bad and rot. Your worm colony will continue to grow as long as they are happy and well fed!

STEP 9: **Harvest the liquid and castings:** The bottom container will catch the juices from the top container; this worm poo juice is like liquid gold! It's extremely nutritious, but it's too strong to apply directly to your plants. Water it down with 10 parts water to 1 part worm juice; you can dilute it up to 20 to 1. Then simply pour it around your plants. Harvest some of the castings as needed, picking out the worms and throwing them back into the bin. Worm castings are literally the worm poop. It looks like wet granules and is distinct from unprocessed soil and compost. Sprinkle the actual compost around your plants and work into the soil for a healthy garden. A little bit goes a long way.

# CHAPTER 11

# PLANTING WITH A PURPOSE

## SELECTING PLANTS THAT ENHANCE YOUR PROPERTY AESTHETICALLY AND FUNCTIONALLY

Plants are versatile and useful in the landscape, from adding color to a space to providing food for your family to screening out unwanted views or creating privacy. Plantings are one of the more affordable things you can do in a yard renovation, plus they soften and naturalize a space and bring a sense of scale to a yard. This chapter will show you how to plant for different purposes, such as to add color; provide privacy; grow fruits and vegetables; or attract flitting butterflies, pollinating bees or birdlife to your yard. A project for a contained planting that will provide all your guacamole ingredients (page 146) will show you how to plant a culinary-themed garden.

## OVERVIEW OF PLANTING

When it comes to planting, remember that you are planting for the future and the plants you put in the ground today are going to be bigger and fuller as they mature. Some plants grow very quickly and can reach full size in a season, such as *Tagetes lemmonii* (Mexican marigold), which grows 3 to 4 feet in a season. Other plants, such as barrel cactus, can take years to grow a few inches. I typically buy smaller annuals and perennials because they grow fairly quickly, but purchase bigger sizes of shrubs, trees and larger landscape plants. For example, don't buy a 6-inch-tall oak tree as the focal piece for your yard because you'll be waiting from 10 to 15 years for it to grow to anything significant. Instead, start with a 24- to 36-inch box or ball-and-burlap tree that is from 6 to 12 feet tall and spend less money on the plants around it.

## COST

The prices of plants vary depending on how fast-growing/slow-growing, common/rare or small/large a plant is. The cost of slow-growing plants, rare plants and large container plants can add up fairly quickly. However, fast-growing plants, common plants and smaller container plants can be quite a bit cheaper and sometimes require more maintenance. You just need to have the patience to let it all grow in.

Other costs to consider are what you need to do to amend your soil (or bring in new soil), whether you'll need a professional or machinery to install large trees and shrubs and how much space you want to fill. When bringing in soil and mulch, consider buying in bulk to save money.

## USING PLANTS IN THE LANDSCAPE

Here are some ways you can use plants in your yard.

**Frame your yard.** If you have a nice view, consider anchoring it with plants on either side for a balanced look within a natural frame.

**Add some privacy.** Screen out your peering neighbors' windows with tall border-screening plants for privacy. Consult your local nursery for suggestions on screening plants. Here are just a few popular shrubs and trees used as screens/hedges:

- Italian cypress (*Cupressus sempervirens*)
- Fern pine (*Afrocarpus gracilior*, formerly known as *Podocarpus*)
- Varigated kohoho (*Pittosporum tenuifolium* 'Marjorie Channon')
- Japanese privet (*Ligustrum japonica*)
- Red-tip photinia (*Photinia fraseri*)
- Purple hoopseed (*Dodonaea purpurea*)
- Clumping bamboo (check locally for varieties in your region)
- Italian buckthorn (*Rhamnus alaternus*)

**Provide shade.** Cool down a yard and overall home temperature by planting a shade tree. Strategically plant a deciduous tree so that you can enjoy shade in the summer and sun in the winter when the tree is leafless.

**Create scale.** Bring a sense of scale to your yard by layering plants. Having taller plants in the back with a front layer of medium-size plants and a border of smaller plants creates a visually interesting space.

**Use container plantings.** Place container plantings in transition spaces, such as the stairs to the deck or next to the front door, to add color, height and interest to areas that can't be planted. Fast-growing perennials or annuals look great spilling out of containers. More architectural plants like aloes, cordylines and agaves make statuesque statements. Plus, you can mix it up from year to year and try new plants or color combinations.

## TYPES OF PLANTS

Plants are grouped into three categories—annual, biannual and perennial—depending on how long they live.

**Annuals.** These plants grow from seeds and die within one year, typically within a season or two. They are popular for their burst of color and are planted each year or as needed. In nature, these plants drop seeds before or after dying and dormant seeds wait until the next growing season to send up shoots and bloom.

**Biannuals.** These plants complete their life cycle in a two-year growing period. The first year is typically for vegetative growth and the second is for flowering and dropping seeds.

**Perennials.** Perennials are plants and shrubs that grow for multiple seasons, making them a popular choice. Some keep their foliage year-round and some have foliage die back, but the same root system keeps the plant alive from season to season. Depending on your climate, some perennials grow as annuals and vice versa. Trees and shrubs are technically perennials, but the term is generally used for any plant that lives longer than two years with little woody growth.

I use mostly perennials when designing gardens because most of my clients don't want to keep planting annuals each year. However, the colorful impact of annuals appeals to people who want to constantly have their garden in peak bloom.

## PLANTING FOR COLOR

Plants are an easy and effective way to add color to the yard, plus they are relatively affordable. They vary in form, size and texture, giving you a lot of attributes to play with. When it comes to adding color to a yard, consider a plant's foliage, flowers and seasonality. While many plants flower in the spring or summer, some flower only in the fall or winter. Select plants that flower in all seasons if you want year-round color and interest. Since plants vary so much from region to region and different climates can affect their flowering season, you'll need to rely on local experts and nurseries to learn what blooms and when in your area.

**Contrasting foliage.** I particularly like working with different foliage colors because they can have much more overall "color" than seasonal flowers. I like to work with contrasting foliage colors in silver/white, burgundy/purple, chartreuse and green.

**Too much of a good thing.** With the exception of cottage-style gardens, mixing too many colors in a small area can look messy. Select two or three colors and plant in waves or rows to get the most impact. This is especially effective for gardens that are viewed from a distance, because the details of the plants lose their impact.

**Color blocking.** This works great in large yards to make them look cohesive and dynamic. Gather plants of a similar color together and combine or contrast them with other plant groupings to make waves of color in the landscape. If you're starting from scratch, lay out all your plants, then walk away and do the "squint test," which is basically squinting your eyes from a distance to see how the colors blend together, and make adjustments if needed. When plants of similar colors are paired together they read as one swath, which can be relaxing on the eye.

**Fast color.** Perennials are great for color and many grow quickly, but annuals are probably the royalty of color, because, let's be honest—why else do they exist? They typically last only one season, so depending on your climate you may have to frequently change them out. Planting with annuals is an active gardening style that needs to be kept up by you or a gardener, so many homeowners prefer to use perennials or plants that live longer than a season. However, annuals can be great for sprucing up an area like an entrance.

**Contemporary look.** Select fewer types of plants, create repetition and space them fairly evenly for a clean, organized and contemporary look.

**Cottage style.** For a wild or cottage garden look, the more variety and randomness, the better.

## PLANTING FOR PRIVACY

Plants are one of the most affordable ways to provide privacy for a property. There are a handful of ways people use plants to screen undesirable views.

**Individual trees.** A single tree can offer a lot of privacy and shade while also being a focal point. However, most trees planted for privacy take years to mature. Avoid planting trees too close to your home's foundation or also to your neighbor's yard if you think they will not enjoy the leaf litter shared under the shade. Some trees soar from 15 to 60 feet or taller if you let them, such as the Italian cypress tree, which is very popular in Mediterranean-style yards. This can create a green wall of separation, especially for a multistory home, and also serves as a windbreak. However, extremely tall trees can dwarf your house in terms of scale and proportion.

**Screening hedges.** These hedges are typically faster-growing shrubs or trees that are placed close together with the intention that they will grow together as one plant. These are most commonly used to line a fence separating neighbors. While some plants will peak above fence height at 6 to 10 feet, many others grow quite a bit taller and some can be maintained at this height by heading and trimming.

**Fast-growing shrubs.** Most people want the fastest growing shrub for the quickest coverage. Many plants do well for this purpose, but the quicker the plant grows, the more you will have to be on top of it to maintain and shape it. Plants like ficus are popular because they are so fast-growing, but they need constant pruning to maintain a manageable size and they also have very aggressive root systems.

Roots usually extend beyond the drip line of a tree/shrub by about two or three times the size of the canopy. However, if you greatly reduce the tree's canopy by maintaining it as a hedge, roots will typically follow suit, as there is a reduction of food and energy available to them. Watering and fertilizing around the natural drip line or the maintained (hedged) drip line is best.

**Screening trellis and vines.** Some vines like bougainvillea and other woody vines are strong enough to hold themselves vertically while providing privacy; other twining, suction/aerial root or tendril forms require more support to reach the heights needed for privacy. Building a trellis or providing a surface such as a fence for them to connect to will allow them to grow vertically.

## FRUIT AND VEGETABLE GARDENS

Growing your own fruits and vegetables is a great idea. It takes time, effort and love, but nothing tastes better than a sweet homegrown tomato. Edible gardens can be fancy and formal or informal and purely functional.

Most edibles thrive in full sun, which means 6 to 8 hours of light a day. Other plants can survive and thrive in lower lighting situations, such as lettuces, kale, spinach and other leafy greens, which can survive on as little as 2 hours of direct sunlight a day, but more sun is ideal. Check your local nursery for plant selections that work in your climate and when to start your plants. Usually the spring after the last frost is the best time to start plants.

> **TIP:** What's *the difference between a fruit and a vegetable? Fruits are the seed-bearing units created from the ovaries of a flower and are intended to be eaten by animals for seed dispersion. Vegetables are any other consumable part of the plant, including roots, leaves and stems.*

## CONSIDERATIONS

- Placing chicken wire or mesh on the bottom of a planter will keep gophers and other soil-digging critters out.
- If birds are a problem, place mesh over the crops while they are fruiting.
- A drip irrigation system will ensure your plants get water even if you can't get to them for a few days. Most fruits and vegetables need regular watering that your climate may or may not provide.
- Raising your garden can save your back if you're not as nimble as you used to be.
- Rotate your crops season to season to help fight off diseases that target certain kinds of plants.
- Enhance your existing soil by adding fertilizer and/or compost and work it into the top 4 to 10 inches of soil depending on the crop.
- When planning a vegetable bed, look for sunny spots that a hose can reach. If you don't plan on tending your garden all the time, don't place it as a focal piece because it will look unkempt for part of the year. Place your garden away from large shrubs and trees to avoid root competition and shade.

## COST

If you start a vegetable garden right from seed and create your own compost, you can have a garden for about $5 plus the water bill. It's easy to spend a lot more on gardens, especially if you have problems with gophers, want a raised bed for ease of use or have poor soil you may choose to build up. There are so many kits and building styles for beds that it really comes down to the cost of materials and preferences.

## RAISED BEDS

Building up? Consider these materials for raised beds.

**Metal.** Corten steel is the best option for longevity, but this would need to be custom made by bolting or welding together metal sheets. This will significantly increase the price, as the material is expensive and the labor is skilled, but the payoff is big in terms of style and functionality.

**Containers.** You can use any planting containers, big or small, to create a raised garden. It's nice to have a few matching containers to pull it together; a lot of variety in containers will look eclectic, which is a nice style too, but it can also look cluttered or messy.

**Lumber.** Lumber is probably the most popular option because it is easy to use, readily available and very versatile. You can make a very modern planter with horizontal runs or a rustic planter with reclaimed wood.

**Concrete.** You can build a custom planter by placing rebar and pouring concrete. Such a planter is strong and bold and has no rot issues—just be sure to leave an open hole for drainage.

**Block/brick/pavers/urbanite.** Use CMU blocks, standard bricks or other stackable units to create a nice solid planter. Mortar them together unless they are designed to be dry stacked.

Don't want to build a vegetable bed? Try mixing edibles and ornamentals in a garden together. There are a few plants that are just as striking as they are yummy. Consider adding kale, artichoke, nasturtium, rhubarb and cabbage to an existing garden for more visual interest and as a filler.

## FRUIT TREES

Fruit trees are a great addition to a landscape, as they add scale and yummy fruits or nuts. Most fruit trees are mature branches grafted onto a young rootstock because young trees can take anywhere from four to eight years to start fruiting. Grafting allows the tree to start fruiting as soon as it's strong enough to support the weight, and sometimes even earlier.

If you have a large yard and are looking to fill some space, add an orchard or a mini orchard. However, if you don't have a lot of space, trees can fill up the yard fast and make it shady and cramped for the rest of your garden. The average fruit tree is between 15 and 40 feet tall and wide when mature, so some people can fit one to three fruit trees in their yard. Luckily, there are options for people who want many trees and don't have a ton of space. Trimming trees down to a manageable size is one way, or you can espalier, or train, a tree or shrub, much like a grape vine on a trellis system, to minimize branching and maximize space and fruit yield. However, this does take regular maintenance. Semi-dwarf and dwarf varieties of fruit trees are also available. Dwarf trees typically grow 6 to 10 feet tall and wide, which is just at or a little above your average fence height, making it a great size for picking fruit. Semi-dwarf trees grow 12 to 15 feet tall and wide, which is a nice size for a small patio.

**TIP:** *Some of my clients collect seeds from their favorite fruit trees and want to plant the seeds with the intent of getting the same harvest. You can certainly plant such seeds, and it's great if you like surprises—good and bad—because there is no guarantee what you're going to get. Think about it like this: you are the product of your mom and dad, but you are neither of them and you have your own unique characteristics. The same goes for a cross-pollinated seed. Since most fruit trees are grafted, you will get the seed of the original rootstock, not the fruiting branches. Plus, you will have to wait years before you get any fruit, whereas a grafted tree from a known variety is a clone of that variety, so you know exactly what to expect and get fruit a lot sooner.*

## CULINARY THEMED GARDENS

Gardening can be fun, especially when you put a theme to it. Try planting a variety of fruits and vegetables for a versatile garden that caters to your favorite dishes, or pick a theme or a dish as the basis of your plant selection. Here are a few of my favorite themed gardens, but don't be afraid to make up your own!

**Pizza garden.** Include tomatoes, garlic, oregano, basil, onion, fennel, thyme, rosemary and any other vegetable topping desired.

**Guacamole garden.** Plant avocado trees, lemon or lime trees, tomatoes, onion and cilantro.

**Cocktail garden.** Include mint, basil, lemon verbena, thyme, tarragon, rosemary, lavender or whatever other herb sounds like it would mix well with the spirit of your choice. These make great windowsill planters.

## PLANTING TO ATTRACT BEES, BIRDS AND BUTTERFLIES

Inviting bees, birds and other wildlife to your yard makes your space come alive. A healthy mix of birds and beneficial bugs can be super rewarding to you and your garden. Singing birds, floating butterflies, lounging lizards and pollinating bees are all great contributors that you should cater to. Here's how.

**Bees.** Bees are the best pollinators, and without them most flowers will not set vital seeds or produce fruit. They are extremely important to our food system and to your garden. Attract them with sunflowers, penstemons, asters and other pollen-abundant flowers.

**Birds.** Birds are attracted to water and nectar from flowers, and some will take up residence in birdhouses if provided. They are great for keeping other insect counts down. Consider installing plants that bloom at different times of the year and/or add a birdfeeder to keep them around.

**Butterflies.** Butterflies float through the yard so effortlessly and beautifully! Consider providing flowering plants that offer nectar for the adult butterflies and leafy shrubs and perennials that the larvae can eat. Use nectar plants native to your area because your local butterfly population will be best adapted to them. Consider planting milkweed, yarrow, echinacea and sage if they thrive in your area.

**Ladybugs.** Not only are they cute, but ladybugs are also awesome at eating up aphids. You can buy ladybugs in the garden department of a hardware or big box store or at a local nursery in the spring and summer.

### CONSIDERATIONS

- Super-manicured yards are less attractive to wildlife than more natural yards, which provide more interesting habitats.
- Use organic products on your garden to avoid harming critters with chemicals.
- Add water to your garden via a birdbath or water feature, especially on hot days.
- Provide food by having a variety of flowering plants and shrubs or trees that produce berries.
- Install rocks that can warm up in the sun and provide a resting place for butterflies and a sunbathing place for lizards.

**TIP:** *Did you know that honeybees are a European import? It's wonderful to have them, but consider attracting native bees, which are used to pollinate your local plant selection. The United States has about 4,000 native bee varieties, and most of them nest in the ground rather than in hives.*

# WHEELBARROW GUACAMOLE GARDEN

## LEVEL: BEGINNER
## COST: $$
## TIME COMMITMENT: 1 AFTERNOON–1 DAY
## PROFESSIONALS NEEDED: NONE
## DIMENSIONS: 2' × 3' PLUS AREA FOR TREES

Avocados are one of my favorite fruits, and one of America's too! It is easy to build a garden and recipes around this wonderful tree. For this project I found a three-in-one avocado tree, which is basically three avocado plants in one container. They are all separate trees, and because they could each grow from 25 to 40 feet tall and wide, they will need to be trimmed to a smaller size so they will be manageable. By combining a few herbs and vegetables in the container next to the avocado tree, you can have all the ingredients needed to make your own guacamole.

## TOOLS

- Gloves
- Hand shovel
- Spade shovel
- Pruning shears
- Hose
- Drill and ¼" metal drill bit
- 2'–3' level

## MATERIALS

- Avocado tree
- 2 bags of 2-cubic-foot potting mix or native soil mixed with compost
- Lemon or lime tree
- An old wheelbarrow, ½ wine barrel or other large planting container
- 2 bags of ½-cubic-foot gravel
- 4' of landscape fabric
- 1-gallon tomato plant
- 4" container cilantro plant
- 4" container onion plant
- Tomato cage
- Organic fruit tree fertilizer
- Two 50-lb bags of ¾" gravel

**STEP 1:** **Select the location of your trees and plant:** Since you will have at least two trees, make sure you place them strategically so that they don't shade areas that you'd like to keep sunny. The avocado will grow large unless maintained via pruning. I selected a semi-dwarf lime because it seemed appropriate for the space given. Avocados and citrus love good drainage, so if possible, place them on a slope, although this is not necessary.

Dig a hole 36 inches wide and just as deep as the soil content in the container of the avocado tree. If digging on a slope, the dirt will be higher on one side and lower on the other. Dig to the depth that matches the measurement on the lower side. The higher ground can be cut back or retained later. Remove the wood on the bottom of the container with pruning shears. Grab a friend or two to help you drop the tree in the hole. Position the tree to your liking, remove the sides of the container and backfill with a mixture of native soil and amended soil.

The lime tree is in a 15-gallon container, which is a lot easier to tackle. Dig a hole twice as wide and just as deep. Position the tree for the best view and then backfill the hole with the amended soil mix. Soak both trees thoroughly.

**STEP 2:** **Drill drainage holes in the wheelbarrow:** The remaining plants are placed in a wheelbarrow (or you can plant them in the ground). I broke this old wheelbarrow on the job site, and instead of throwing it away, I used it as a cute container for the garden. The wheelbarrow already has one hole in it from wear and tear, but it needs more to drain properly. Drill three more holes with a ¼-inch metal drill bit.

**STEP 3:** **Add a layer of gravel:** Fill the wheelbarrow with the gravel or about 2 inches of ¾-inch angular gravel to help with drainage.

**STEP 4:** **Add a layer of landscape fabric:** Place a piece of landscape fabric over the gravel to separate it from the soil. This helps keep the soil from clogging the drainage holes and losing soil every time the plants are thoroughly watered.

**STEP 5:** **Add soil:** Fill the wheelbarrow with an amended soil or potting soil until it is about two-thirds full. Make sure the soil is level.

**STEP 6:** **Plant:** Lay out the plants in a pleasing arrangement. I placed the tomato, the tallest plant, in the back and filled in with the cilantro and onion. Place a cage on the tomato plant to encourage it to grow upright. Water deeply and make sure the soil doesn't dry out. Before you know it, you'll be able to make your own guacamole!

## AVOCADO PLANTS

This avocado is three trees in one container, with a Hass, a Pinkerton and a Fuerte, so there is sure to be plenty of fruit! Although avocados will fruit on their own, they do much better when paired with an avocado that flowers at a different time, thereby increasing pollination opportunities. The avocado flower has both male (produces pollen) and female (receives pollen) parts, and they open at different times. Type "A" flowering avocados open in the morning as female and close by late morning/early afternoon; they remain closed until the afternoon of the second day, when they open as male. Type "B" flowering avocados open as female in the afternoon of the first day and then open as male in the morning of the second day.

### TYPE "A" FLOWERING AVOCADOS

- Hass -
- Gwen
- Lamb Hass
- Pinkerton
- Reed

### TYPE "B" FLOWERING AVOCADOS

- Bacon
- Fuerte
- Sir Prize
- Ettinger
- Sharwil
- Walter Hole

# CHAPTER 12

# BUILT ELEMENTS AND ENHANCING FEATURES

## FUNCTIONAL FINAL TOUCHES AND DECORATIVE PIECES

A residential landscape is a unique union of natural and built space. A garden can stand on its own, but adding built or decorative features can enhance the functionality of your yard, define a space and contribute to the overall aesthetic. This chapter will explore the many ways you can enhance your yard with custom-made or purchased items like benches, planter boxes and potting tables. Adding decorative items such as cushions, potted plants and sculpture or other art is a gratifying way to bring personal flair to your space. And the right lighting, whether installed by a professional or a string of LED bistro lights, can enhance a space dramatically and extend the yard's usability far into the night. The projects in this chapter—a tile mosaic potting table, a vertical garden wall (all the rage right now), a U-shaped vegetable garden and a simple garden bridge—will definitely bring your yard to the next level.

# DÉCOR

Landscape décor takes your yard from ordinary to extraordinary. Whether your yard is decorated for a one-time event or incorporates permanent embellishments, these elements will make your yard comfortable, beautiful and a natural extension of your indoor space.

**Outdoor cushions** are a must-have in most of my landscapes. Whether they are custom made or purchased, they bring comfort and a lot of color to the yard. Be sure to use outdoor fabric and take care to protect cushions from the elements to extend their life.

**Potted plants** are a great way to soften a hardscape space and reference the rest of the yard. It can be about the plant, the planter or both. There are many architecturally interesting planters available that can highlight the style of your yard. Be sure to pick the appropriate plant for the amount of sun or shade it will get.

**Sculpture and art** provide focal points and conversation pieces that reflect your personality.

**Candle holders, fixtures and other decorative pieces** are the small accents that make a big difference. You can find a plethora of items made from metal, ceramic, concrete or glass that will all hold up well outside and give your yard a finished look. Make your own accents or visit local local antique/thrift stores, home good stores or online sites.

## METAL BALLS

Decorating with spheres is always a good idea in my book. I couldn't find metal balls in the size or at the price point I wanted, so I had these balls assembled out of stainless steel salad bowls. While they are merely tack welded, they are the perfect touch to step this yard up and reinforce the design elements.

## LIGHTING

Landscape lighting can have a huge influence on your yard. It greatly extends your evening usage and makes your outdoor space inviting and functional. There are ways to achieve a great lighting scheme on all budgets, from simply plugging in bistro lights to placing solar path lights to installing more permanent fixtures. The most popular outdoor lighting sources are halogen, incandescent, LED and solar.

LEDs are the most popular professional lights on the market because they last on average about twenty years and use a fraction of the energy of other lights. LEDs were once shunned for their low light levels and blue/green hues, but modern LED chips are much improved and warmer tones are now achievable. The quality of the lights and the housing units vary quite a bit, and that greatly affects the cost. I put in only professional-grade landscape lights that are made of aluminum, copper or brass and on average cost from $75 to $200 or more per fixture, not including labor or the transformer. It is not untypical to see a lighting estimate for $5,000 to $10,000 on a yard. I try to keep the cost between $2,000 and $3,500 for many of my clients and just highlight a few important features to get them started and then they can easily add more lights as their budget permits in the future, if they choose. Of course, this puts lighting out of reach for many people, but you can also expect the lights to be hassle-free and reliable for a long time. A lighting designer, landscape designer or contractor can be helpful with the layout and light selections, which is not a bad idea if you are making the investment with professional-grade lights. In fact, a supplier is often happy to offer a demonstration if you are planning on placing a minimum order.

Minimal lighting to highlight features and walkways in the yard is also an option. Be careful not to go overboard and make it look like Disneyland: your neighbors won't appreciate it and neither will wildlife. Consider lighting up pathways, destination points and significant trees or other interesting or key features in the yard.

## CONSIDER THE FOLLOWING FOR THE LOWER END OF THE BUDGET SPECTRUM

- Plug-in lighting features are great if you have an exterior outlet. If not, an electrician can install a GIF outlet for a few hundred dollars.
- Outdoor bistro lights set a romantic and festive mood and are easy, as they just plug in.
- Candles are great for ambience and citronella candles can help deter mosquitoes.
- Solar lights are easy to install, but make sure they get enough rays during the day to charge them.
- Battery-operated lights are a good option for short periods of time, and are especially useful if you don't have access to an exterior outlet or want something portable.

# MOSAIC POTTING TABLETOP

**LEVEL: BEGINNER–INTERMEDIATE**
**COST: $$**
**TIME COMMITMENT: AFTERNOON + NEXT DAY GROUTING**
**PROFESSIONALS NEEDED: OPTIONAL PLUMBER (TO HOOK UP WATER)**
**DIMENSIONS: 6' × 27"**

A potting table can be very useful in a garden, and this one in particular came together from the scraps of my childhood swing set. The swing set was no longer functional and it was disassembled for scraps and reassembled by my buddy and builder John Serbian as a great practical piece in the yard. The sink was taken from one of my client's trash piles, and now I can't wait to use it to wash my vegetables. Any sort of sturdy table will work for this application, as long as the sides can be framed up to hold a cement board and tiles and it can hold the weight of the new decorative top. Use cement board for the base of the tiles because it does not expand and contract the way wood does, which will compromise the adhesion of the tiles or pop them off. You can use scrap tiles, broken ceramic plates or glass tiles.

(continued)

# TOOLS

- Measuring tape
- Miter saw
- Circular saw
- Utility knife
- Straightedge
- Saw
- Drill
- Rubber gloves
- Tile cutters
- Nippers
- Hose
- Scrub brush
- 5-gallon bucket
- Trowel
- Small hand pick
- Paintbrush or toothbrush
- Sponge
- Cloth

# MATERIALS

- Reclaimed counter-height table (34"–36") (or build your own)
- Two 2" × 4" × 10' cedar boards cut to the following dimensions:
    - Two cut to 6' with mitered vertical edges (or to the dimensions of your table)
    - Two cut to 27" with vertical edges (or to the dimensions of your table)
- 3' × 5' × ¼" cement board, cut to measure the tabletop (or use two, if not putting in a sink)
- Three 1' × 1' mirror tiles
- Three 2" × 2" × 10' pieces of redwood
- One 1-lb box of 1½" drywall screws
- One 1-lb box of 2½" exterior screws
- Tiles, square footage of your tabletop plus 10 percent
- 50-lb bag of thinset
- 25-lb bag of colored sanded grout
- Sink (optional)

**STEP 1:** **Prepare the table:** Find a simple table or build your own. Build a vertical mitered frame around the tabletop with 2 × 6s and a ¾-inch lip above the edge to frame the cement board, tiles and thinset. (Optional: If you would like to place a sink, you can find some nice affordable ones at resale yards. Measure the base under the lip of the sink, then use a circular saw to cut out the dimensions, leaving at least 2 to 3 inches on all sides. You'll need to add a 2 × 4 frame on the underside of the counter to hold the extra weight of the sink and screw it into the surrounding frame.)

**STEP 2:** **Prepare the cement base:** Measure the cement board to be fit inside the frame. Cut the cement board with a utility knife and a straightedge to the correct dimensions and cut for any amenities, such as a sink. Attach the cement board to the tabletop with drywall screws.

**STEP 3:** **Select and lay out your tiles:** This is the fun part. Put on rubber gloves when working with scrap tiles, as the edges are sharp, and figure out a layout that you like. I struggled at first with these uniquely shaped tiles, but I welcomed the challenge and love how it turned out.

**STEP 4:** **Cut the tiles to fit:** Use the tile cutters and nippers to cut the tiles to fit. Try to keep the grout spaces between ⅛ and ¼ inch and not any bigger than ½ inch. Make sure to leave about a ¼-inch gap between the wood frame and tile for grout.

**STEP 5:** **Clean the surface:** Use a hose and scrub brush to clean off all the debris from the tabletop surface. Make sure the top is not sopping wet; let it dry out a little before placing the tiles.

**STEP 6:** **Attach the tiles:** In a 5-gallon bucket, mix thinset to a thick but smooth consistency, let sit for 10 minutes, then remix. Use a trowel to apply thinset on the back of the tile and attach each piece as you go. Try not to get thinset on top or high up on the sides of the tile.

STEP 7: **Keep it clean:** As you're setting tiles, be conscious of messy or bulging thinset, because this will show as white when you grout. Use a hand pick to scrape out any thinset that is too high so you have room for the grout. Let the tiles set up overnight before grouting.

STEP 8: **Select and mix the grout:** The grout color is part of the design, so pick a color that will enhance your tiles. I never use white outside because it is bound to get dirty, so I almost always use some variation of brown or gray, but don't be afraid to go bold and use red, blue or black, as it can really make the tiles pop . . . if that's what you're going for. Mix the sanded grout in a 5-gallon bucket to a thick almond-butter consistency.

STEP 9: **Clean the joints:** Clean out all the joints with a brush to remove any dirt or debris that will prevent the grout from adhering.

STEP 10: **Apply the grout:** Use a damp sponge to scoop out a small amount of grout and push it into the joints in a circular motion. Use a clean part of the sponge after each wipe and wash off your sponge as you go. After the joints are filled, let the tiles haze over with a film of residue.

STEP 11: **Wipe it down:** With a clean, damp sponge, wipe off the grout residue, making sure to use a clean part of the sponge every time. Wash your sponge often. (Never clean concrete in a sink because it can clog your pipes.) Be careful not to pull out any of the grout from the joints.

STEP 12: **Buff it out:** After the residue hazes over, again, use a cloth to buff out the haze. It should look nice and shiny now!

STEP 13: **Add a decorative back (optional):** Using 2 × 2-inch redwood lumber, cut mitered frames for the 1 × 1-inch mirrored tiles. Create a backing for the frames with cut fence boards and use a ½-inch piece of trim to secure the mirrors in the frame. Attach two 5-foot 2 × 2s between the 4 × 4 posts of the stand and then attach your mirrors with 2½-inch screws.

You'll enjoy using this potting table to wash all your fruits and vegetables, and aesthetically it will be a showpiece in your yard.

# VERTICAL GARDEN WALL

**LEVEL: BEGINNER-INTERMEDIATE**
**COST: $$$**
**TIME COMMITMENT: 1–2 DAYS**
**PROFESSIONALS NEEDED: NONE**
**DIMENSIONS: 11' × 9"**

Pocket vertical garden bags are one of my favorite methods for a green wall because it is simple and effective. I helped my buddy Navid Mostatabi (Envision Landscape Architecture) with this project for his client, who wanted a nice focal point from his window along the narrow side of his home. The wooden support that Navid created is beautiful and has a low profile, making it great for a tight space.

While this system is set for drip irrigation, you can also hand water if you don't have an irrigation system to tie into. Because these pockets hold only a little soil, the plants can dry out more rapidly than when they are in the ground, so make sure you can hand water two or three times a week or so during the warmer seasons. Also expect to edit and change out plants as needed for the different seasons because some plants will outgrow the pockets.

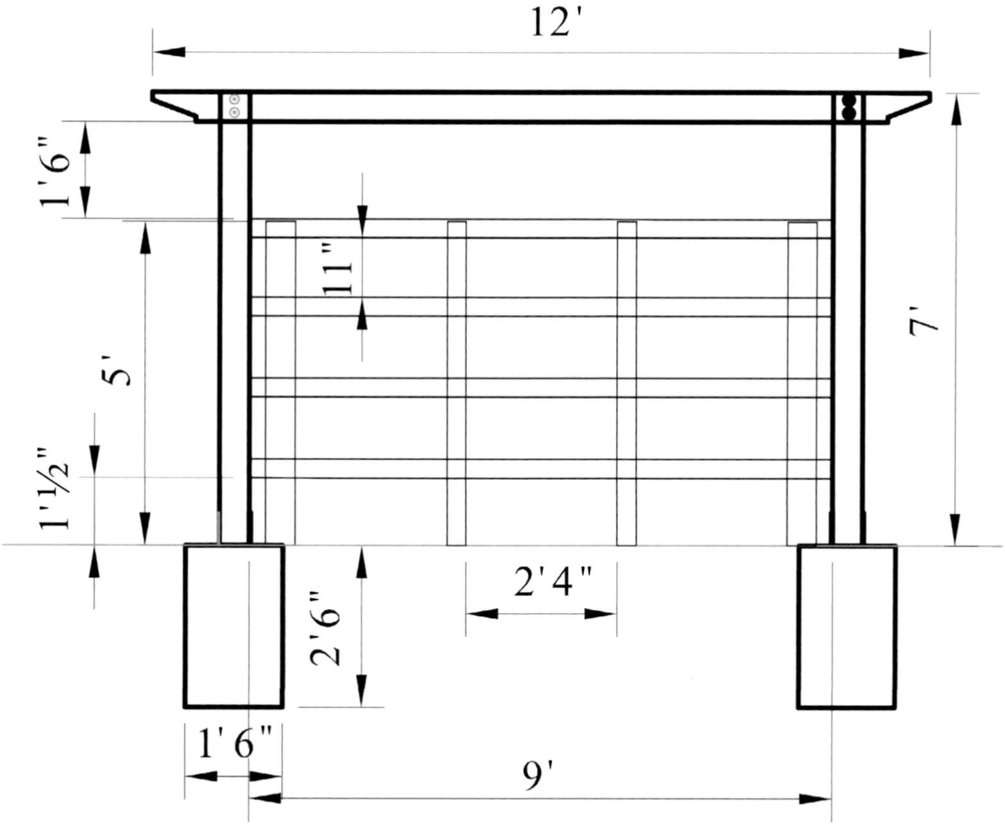

## TOOLS

- String line
- Wheelbarrow
- Shovel
- Circular saw
- 3'–6' level
- Drill and ½" × 10" drill bit
- Garden gloves
- Trowel
- Level

## MATERIALS

### WALL

- Two 6" × 6" metal post bases
- Two 2" × 6" × 12' cedar boards with detail cuts on ends 1" from the bottom, 1½" from the top and 8" in from the edge
- Four 2" × 4" × 10' cedar boards cut to 9' each
- Two 6" × 6" × 8' cedar pressure-treated boards
- One 2" × 6" × 12' cut to make two 5' pieces
- One 2" × 4" × 12' cut to make two 5' pieces
- Four 4½" × 10" through bolts
- Four 4½" × 1½" diameter washers
- Sixteen 50-lb bags of concrete
- One 1-lb box of 2½" screws

### PLANTER

- Three 5-pocket fabric garden pockets (I recommend WoollyPockets)
- 12 fasteners (provided in kit)
- Four 2-cubic-foot bags of potting soil
- Fifteen 1-gallon plants
- ¼" spaghetti drip tubing (optional)

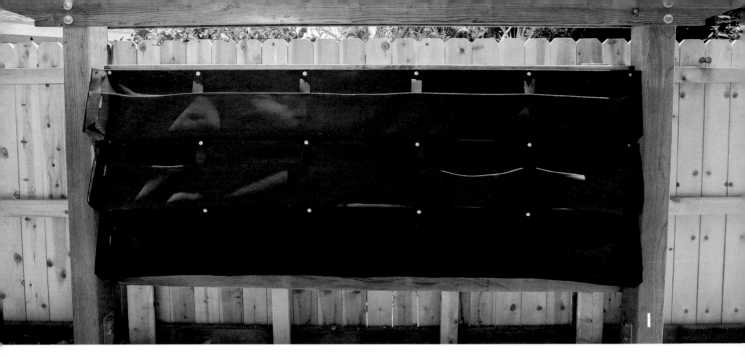

STEP 1: **Build the structure and attach the bags:** This support structure is simple and sleek; built out of 6 × 6-inch posts and 2 × 6-inch and 2 × 4-inch stringers, it offers the perfect area to attach garden pockets. Here is how this was built.

**Set the brackets:** Dig two 30-inch-deep 18 × 18-inch holes; mix and pour concrete. Set the post bases while the concrete is wet and use a string line to make sure the posts are in line with each other. Wait 24 hours and then set your 6×6 posts in the bases with the included screws.

**Build the frame:** Cut the 8-foot posts down to 7 feet with a circular saw and then attach the two 12-foot 2 × 6-inch boards to the top with the lag bolts and washers. Use a drill bit first to predrill your holes. Start attaching one side, then use a level before attaching the other side.

**Attach the runners:** Attach the 9-foot boards between the 6 × 6-inch posts. The first runner starts 18 inches down from the top and is attached with 2½-inch screws toenailed in from the top and the bottom. The next row starts 11 inches below the first so that the pockets will overlap when installed (they will be 13 inches from grommet to grommet). Repeat to attach the other two runners.

**Add support:** Since these pockets will be heavy when filled with soil, they can start pulling the runners down. To prevent sagging, add four support boards: two 5-foot-long 2 × 6-inch boards spaced about 3 inches in from the post and two 5-foot-long 2 × 4-inch boards spaced about 2 feet apart on the inside, running perpendicular across the back. These support boards attach to the pressure-treated runner that is attached to the fence (or attached to the structure if you aren't placing it against a fence). Secure each runner to the support boards with 2½-inch screws.

**Attach the pockets:** The grommets are spaced every 22 inches on the bags. Measure 1 inch down from the top of the first runner and predrill the holes, then add the screws and attach the grommets.

You can build a similar structure or create something unique of your own. We used three five-pocket units that hold about 2 cubic feet of soil and are 15 inches tall and 112 inches wide. You can customize your wall to the pocket sizes or buy individual pockets as needed to fit the space. Hang the bag by slipping the grommets onto the screws.

**STEP 2:** **Select and lay out the plants:** Your plant selection will vary greatly on whether you have full sun, part sun or no sun. It is best to choose a variety of plants that grow upright and cascade down so you can cover the bags above and the bags below. You can choose plants of all sizes. This style of gardening requires regular pruning as it grows in. Place the plants in the pockets to find a layout that you like and adjust as needed.

**STEP 3:** **Add the soil:** Fill the pockets about halfway with potting soil.

**STEP 4:** **Plant the plants:** Fit the plants into the pockets. We used three plants per pocket, which makes the wall very full because the plants grow in quickly and robustly. All vertical walls are going to need maintenance, pruning and removing of plants as they grow. Keep the soil level about 2 inches below the lip of the pocket after all the plants are installed.

**STEP 5:** **Run the irrigation (optional):** These pockets have a sleeve sewn into the top of the bags for spaghetti drip tubing to run through. Having this option in a vertical garden is great because these can dry out and heat up a lot quicker than plants in the ground. If you have an irrigation system already, you can connect your drip lines to this with some adaptations. There are also kits that you can purchase that hook up to a hose bib for an easier installation.

Enjoy this beautiful backdrop for years to come, and add and remove plants as needed to keep it looking fresh.

# U-SHAPED VEGETABLE GARDEN

**LEVEL: BEGINNER TO INTERMEDIATE**
**COST: $$**
**TIME COMMITMENT: 1 DAY**
**PROFESSIONALS NEEDED: NONE**
**DIMENSIONS: 8' × 9' U-SHAPE**

Garden beds make any yard come alive, and the best part about having a raised bed is that it looks attractive even in the off-season because it defines and organizes the space in the yard. A simple U-shaped bed gives you maximum growing space with all-around access. Adding a cute little bench to the cap and some decorative diamonds can really dress it up! This large garden can be a focal piece or complement other features in the yard. Plan to hand water unless you want to install an irrigation system (I prefer drip).

BEFORE

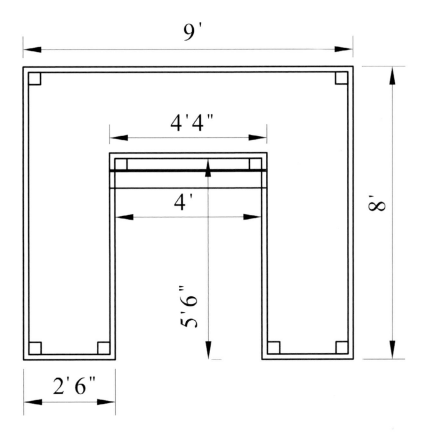

## TOOLS

- Measuring tape
- Pencil
- Miter saw or circular saw
- 2'–3' level
- Shovel
- Rake
- Hand tamper
- Impact driver or drill and socket bit
- String line
- Speed square
- Stakes
- Clamps
- Hose with multispray nozzle
- Finish nail gun (optional, if not using deck screws)

## MATERIALS

- Three 2" × 12" × 10' boards, two cut into 9' and one cut into two 51" pieces
- Two 4" × 4" × 8' redwood boards, cut into eight 22" pieces
- Eight 2" × 12" × 8' boards
  - Four whole
  - Four cut to 5' 6"
- Six 2" × 4" × 10' boards (wait and cut based on your actual dimensions in case they vary a little) (cap)
- Two 2" × 4" × 8' boards, each miter cut to make twelve 15" pieces (diamonds)
- One 2" × 6" × 10', cut to two 51" boards (bench)
- ⅓ cubic yard of ¾" gravel
- Thirty-two 3½" × ⅜" lag bolts and washers
- ⅜" drill bit
- 3½ cubic yards of garden soil
- One 1-lb box of 2½" deck screws

STEP 1: **Select your location:** Pick a nice sunny area that is fairly level and easy to get to.

This garden box will fit in a 9 × 9-foot space; you can adjust yours to be bigger or smaller depending on your area. However, I don't recommend going smaller than 30 inches (2½ feet) for the arms, as it gets too tight to plant two rows of veggies.

STEP 2: **Select and cut your lumber:** I used "merch" redwood, which is really rough and imperfect redwood, as it drops the price significantly and works great for a rough, rustic veggie bed. I recommend using raw redwood or cedar for planters. Never use pressure-treated lumber for a vegetable garden. With a miter saw, cut all your lumber to the specified dimensions above or adjust for your own space.

STEP 3: **Grade your level:** Most sites are going to need some slight leveling or be cut and filled to get an even surface. You have two options: dig out the high areas and transfer the soil to the low areas or build up the whole space with the ¾-inch gravel. Compact it with a hand tamper and use a rake to level it out.

STEP 4: **Start with the back:** Since we are placing this planter against a fence, start with the long back pieces by assembling them on the ground. To do this, take one 9-foot board and line it up with one of the 22-inch 4 × 4 posts. The bottoms should line up square and overhang the side by 1¾ inches or by the width of your lumber, as a sidepiece will fit in there later. Use two 3½-inch lag bolts and washers to attach about 2½ inches down from each edge so that they are roughly in the center of the 4 × 4. Predrill holes as shown in step 5 and secure as shown in step 6. Attach a second 9-foot board above the first in the same manner and then attach a second 22-inch 4 × 4 post on the other side, still leaving a 1¾-inch gap on the end.

Now take an 8-foot 2 × 12-inch board and slide it in to match the bottom board height and into the overhanging space. Secure with the same bolt and washers as described above and repeat on the other side.

**STEP 5:** **Predrill the holes:** Use a ⅜-inch drill bit to predrill your lumber as you go before inserting screws, which will help prevent splitting and will guide your lag bolt into the lumber.

**STEP 6:** **Secure the lumber:** Use a socket bit with an impact driver to secure the two pieces of lumber together with lag bolts and washers on each end. Lag bolts are heavy-duty screws that are best for securing thick lumber.

**STEP 7:** **Run a string line and add the sides:** Prop up the back and make sure that it is sitting level. Secure a string line to the back and pull the line so that it is perfectly perpendicular, using a speed square to check that it is 90 degrees. Secure it to another structure or tie it to a stake in the ground. Take one of your 8-foot boards and slide it into the 1¾-inch overhanging edge, referencing the string line, and secure with lag bolts.

**STEP 8:** **Attach the front:** Using a clamp or an extra pair of hands, attach a 30-inch 4 × 4 front piece to one of the sides. Clamps are great if you need to force a warped board into place.

STEP 9: **Check your level:** Use a level to verify that you're building straight up and then attach the 30" piece to the 4 × 4 post with bolts.

STEP 10: **Add the top layer of wood:** Drop in the top side pieces, predrill and secure with bolts, as you did in steps 5 and 6, except this time you're building in place. The top layer will sit a few inches taller than the 4 × 4, so that when you fill with soil you can cover the top of the 4 × 4 to make it disappear.

STEP 11: **Finish the box:** Continue building the box by finishing the "legs," or the 8-foot sides, the 30-inch front and the 5-foot-6-inch inner side on both sides of the planter. Your 4 × 4 posts on the inner part of the planter should sit flush with the end of the 5-foot-6-inch boards. Then take the 51-inch 2 × 12 boards and attach them to the 4 × 4 posts, closing the box so that you have a U-shape.

STEP 12: **Add gravel and dirt:** Add a 2-inch layer of gravel to the bottom to help with drainage. Then fill the box up with 3½ cubic yards of garden soil. After filling the box a few inches deep, use a hose to mist the soil down to help compact it and make it moist for your new plants, and use a rake to spread it around. Repeat this step until the container is filled to about 2 inches below the lip and the soil just covers the 4 × 4 inside posts. For this amount of soil it's probably easiest to get it delivered in bulk from a landscape supply store, or you can buy it in bags, but it will be more expensive that way.

STEP 13: **Add a cap and bench seat:** Secure your two 2 × 6 × 51-inch boards on the inside corner of the bench, spacing them ½ inch apart. Then take your 10-foot 2 × 4-inch boards and line up a board so that it is flush with the inside edge of the top vertical 2 × 12-inch boards. This will leave an overhang on the outside by about 1½ inches. Make miter cuts on a miter saw to get nice, clean 45-degree angles where the boards overlap in the corners. Use a drill and 2½-inch exterior screws to secure the cap in each corner and about every 12 inches along the long sides and about every 6 feet on the short 30-inch pieces.

STEP 14: **Add a decorative backdrop:** Use two 8-foot 2 × 4-inch boards and miter cut 12 at 15 inches long to make three separate diamonds. Using 4 pieces per diamond, attach by using a 2½-inch exterior screw on the side. Measure out from the center of the planter and mark 18 inches above on the fence; attach your center diamond using exterior deck screws or a finish nail gun. Space out the other two diamonds about 12 inches away on both sides and secure the same way. Now get planting!

## MODERN CONCRETE AND WOOD BENCH

This simple, modern bench is a functional piece but also drives a strong modern design style throughout the yard. The concrete corners were formed and poured all at once with a gray-colored concrete patio. We built them 18 inches tall and left 4-inch-deep by 11-inch by 6-inch notches for the 4 × 4-inch cedar planks to sit inside. Using a painted angle iron brace attached with redheads to the concrete and with screws to the wood, we were able to secure each of the planks ½ inch apart so that no hardware is visible from the top. While simple in theory, getting everything lined up just right is the key to a perfect modern bench. Placing decorative pea gravel raised the ground level so that the benches sat at a standard 16 inches tall. Finishing the space off with a matching lumber coffee table creates a modern and functional entertaining area that ties in perfectly with the other elements of the yard.

# SIMPLE GARDEN BRIDGE

**LEVEL: BEGINNER**
**COST: $**
**TIME COMMITMENT: 1 AFTERNOON**
**PROFESSIONALS NEEDED: NONE**
**DIMENSIONS: 3' × 10'**

This is a super easy and fun project that doesn't take a lot of skills and uses very basic materials. You can complete this project in a long afternoon. You'll have a functional and cute bridge to connect pathways or cross over a creek bed.

## TOOLS

- Measuring tape
- Pencil
- Speed square or straightedge
- Miter saw or circular saw
- Clamps
- Jigsaw (or circular saw)
- Drill
- Sander
- Paintbrush or roller
- ½" spacer (make one from a scrap piece of lumber)

## MATERIALS

- Two 2" × 10" × 10' pressure-treated boards
- Three 2" × 4" × 10' pressure-treated boards, each cut to four 27" pieces for a total of 12 pieces
- Eleven 2" × 4" × 8' cedar or redwood boards, cut to thirty-two 32" pieces
- One 1-lb box of 2½" exterior screws
- Stain or sealer

**STEP 1: Select your location:** A bridge is a nice accent for any yard. Consider placing one over a creek bed or to break up a long pathway. A good width is from 2½ to 4 feet. This garden bridge is 32 inches wide by 10 feet long.

**STEP 2: Mark your curve:** Use a measuring tape to mark the center on one piece of 10-foot 2 × 10-inch pressure-treated lumber and then mark 2½ feet on either side of the center mark. Using a speed square or a straightedge, measure 5 inches up from the center mark; this is the apex of your curve, and where your line meets the bottom 2½ feet out to each side is where the curve starts/ends. Measure 1 foot out from the center mark on either side and mark 4 inches from the bottom edge. Continue making these marks until you can connect the dots to create a curve that you like. You can also use a few pieces of paper taped together as a stencil to trace your curve.

**STEP 3:** **Cut your lumber:** With a miter or circular saw, cut all of the 2 × 4s to 27 inches per the material list. Take your marked-out 2 × 10 board, secure it to a stable surface with clamps and start cutting the curve using a jigsaw. Try to make one nice clean cut, as the scrap piece is needed to complete this project. Once one board is cut, place it on top of the other (unmarked) board and use it to trace out the same curve.

**STEP 4:** **Attach the arches:** Now that you've cut your arches, take the smaller curve cut out from the bottom of the board and place it on the top edge of the board. Center it and secure it with screws on the ends. The two screws on the ends aren't enough to hold the pieces together for the long run, so you will need a brace or a "mending bracket" to hold them together. Attach two of the 27-inch 2 × 4-inch pressure-treated pieces on the inside center of each board with eight 2½-inch screws as a brace to hold the two pieces together.

**STEP 5:** **Center the braces:** Use the remaining ten 27-inch boards to connect the two arches. Start on the top of the arch about 4 inches from the edge and attach with screws so that the top is flush with the top of the bridge. Secure six of these in this fashion along the top, with three on each side. Take the last four 27-inch boards and attach them so they are flush with the bottom of the frame, staggered between the supports above. You should have two on each side.

STEP 6: **Sand and stain:** Sand all the edges of the cedar boards so they are rounded, with no sharp corners and frayed ends. I like to stain my lumber before I attach it together, so I know I've covered it on all sides for the best protection. I used a semitransparent colored stain to bring out the grain and give it a nice warm tone.

STEP 7: **Attach the top:** This is the fun part. You've put together your base, so now it's time to attach the top boards. I cut ½-inch spacers out of scrap lumber to keep a consistent spacing between each of the 32 cedar boards. There is a 1-inch overhang on either side. Attach the boards directly to the arches with two screws on each side, 1½ inches in from the edge. Start from the center of the arch and work your way down on each side at the same time.

# CHAPTER 13

# MULCH, LAWN AND OTHER GROUND COVERS

## NATURE'S NATURAL BLANKET

Ground cover can range from lawn to mulch to sprawling plants. They offer a beautiful and affordable way to cover a lot of space and enhance your yard. Mulch is typically loose organic or nonorganic material that is used to cover open space. Lawns are used to create open green space and also as a filler or as a default with open space. Vegetative ground covers are typically low-growing, wide-spreading plants that cover an area; some are suitable for walking on while others are better for viewing and greening up or adding color to an area.

You can find all of these ground cover options at landscape supply yards or nurseries. Big box stores also supply ground covers in bagged or smaller quantities. If you want to cover a large area, consider buying in bulk to save money (landscape yards usually deliver).

Mulches, lawn and vegetative ground covers are all relatively affordable, especially when compared to hardscape. However, the more affordable an element in a landscape, the more upkeep it usually requires. All of these will need regular maintenance and touching up from time to time.

Installing ground covers and laying mulch or sod/seed are all within the realm of DIY and can offer a big impact in terms of dressing up or finishing off a site. This chapter will explore the options for all kinds of ground covers and the project on page 176 will show you how to install edging and lay sod for a clean, finished look.

## MULCH

Mulch is an organic or nonorganic ground covering that protects the top layer of soil, keeps moisture in the soil and discourages weeds. It can vary from fine organic matter to wood chips to decorative glass.

Let me put this into context for you. Imagine you were lying outside completely naked and fully exposed to the sun all day. How would your skin feel? What would it look like? Dry, cracked, burnt? Well, the same thing happens to your soil when it has no cover. The sun sucks the moisture out, heats it up and dries it out.

Nature typically takes care of itself. Have you ever walked through a forest? Is the ground bare? Generally, no! It usually has fallen leaves, branches, debris from other plants and vegetative ground cover. This protective layer retains moisture in the soil, adds nutrients and minerals from decomposing organic matter and provides habitat for critters. In typical modern landscaping methods, we try to mimic natural mulch with tree bark, rocks, rubber mulch and other methods that are aesthetically pleasing. Some options are better than others depending on your needs. Here are some of the most common types of mulch used.

### NATURAL MULCH: FREE

Yay! Your yard creates this natural layer already with leaf debris and other fallen plant material. Unless you are trying to go for a different look under tree canopies, I encourage you to let nature do its thing. It's cheaper and requires less maintenance than trying to blow or rake the leaves off. However, if you are trying to maintain a lawn under a tree canopy, leaving the leaf debris is not an option. Gather your leaves and compost them elsewhere!

### ORGANIC NON-WOOD CHIP MULCH: $

There are a number of organic materials that can be used as mulch. The best thing about organic mulches is that they most closely resemble the natural system. Organic matter decomposes and adds nutrients to the soil. You will see people use straw, shredded leaves, grass clippings, coconut coir, pine needles and even shredded newspaper. This is not technically seen in landscaped yards, but often seen in vegetable gardens.

### WOOD CHIPS/BARK: $–$$

There are so many different types of wood chips and bark depending on where you live. This is the most popular form of mulch. The cost can range from free to quite pricey for some of the more processed or rare types. If you are looking to obtain mulch on a budget, check out your local greenery at the landfill or contact local arborists. These free or low-cost mulches are kind of a grab bag—a little less uniform in size, color and shape—but work just as well. If you want a uniform clean "dressing" mulch, you can purchase it from a landscape supply store by the yard or from a big box store in bags.

### RUBBER MULCH: $$

Rubber mulch is typically made from recycled tires. It is great for high-traffic areas with kids, and you can get it in a variety of colors, which is pretty fun. Rubber mulch runs a little more expensive but lasts a long time. I recommend this for people spaces more than plant spaces, as it doesn't decompose to add nutrients back to the soil.

### ROCK MULCH: $$–$$$

Using rocks as mulch adds a completely different aesthetic. There are so many options, sizes, textures and colors form which to choose. From round pea gravel to angular ¾-inch stone to smooth river rock and dark Mexican beach pebble, there is something for every look. However, the rocks will absorb more heat, which can be great for some plants and bad for others.

### GLASS MULCH: $$$$

This is one of my favorite decor touches, as the color and beauty you get from glass mulch are incomparable. Since it is so expensive, it doesn't make sense to use it on a large scale (unless you're Madonna!). But in smaller areas and in pots it can be the perfect touch to add year-round pizzazz and color.

Keep in mind, gardens grow and mulches decompose. Expect to replace your organic mulches at least once a year. Maintaining a 2- to 4-inch layer will garner you the most benefits.

### BENEFITS OF MULCHING

- Discourages weeds
- Maintains moisture in the soil (requires less watering)
- Regulates temperatures, cooler in the summer and warmer in the winter
- Creates a "finished" or maintained landscape look
- Protects the soil, your plants' home
- Organic varieties add nutrients and minerals to the soil
- Creates a beneficial habitat for critters

### LAWNS

Almost everyone loves the idea of having a lawn. And why not? They are pleasant and offer a nice outdoor carpet that works great as a filler or as an area for lounging or for activities. Depending on where you live, growing grass can be the easiest or most challenging part of the landscape. In many areas, grass naturally grows just fine with the local soil type and rain patterns. There is still a decent amount of maintenance and upkeep to make it a "manicured" lawn, but nature is on your side in these areas.

If you live in an arid or nonnatural area for lawn, you're going to need to do a lot more preparation and maintenance to keep your lawn alive and looking good. In fact, lawn might not even be a good choice for your yard, depending on what you're trying to accomplish. Many people are moving away from lawns, which is wise in arid areas. There are a lot of other options, such as adding a patio space, garden bed or lawn alternatives, usually low-growing, water-saving ground covers. If you don't plan on actually using the lawn, then I would guide you away from installing one. However, if there is a purpose and use for a lawn, then small, responsibly maintained spaces can add a lot of green and free space for families to enjoy.

As long as there have been lawns, there has been a connection to social status. The traditional lawn is largely influenced by the British and Scottish, because they have a natural environment that supports widespread growth of grass. Since maintaining a manicured lawn was reserved only for the wealthy who could afford this luxury, the lawn has long been associated with wealth, well-being and social status. However, with the invention of the lawn mower and with people moving to the suburbs, lawns became one of the most sought-after additions right after the garage and picket fence.

Times are changing, however, and in areas where lawns don't grow easily or naturally, people are trying instead to work with their natural environment. Lawns are losing popularity in many areas because of maintenance issues and high water usage. Still, in areas not struggling with drought or where lawns grow easily, the green carpet is going strong.

**Grass.** There are many options when it comes to choosing grass, but the most important factor is your local climate, the type of usage the lawn will get and sun/shade needs. Contact your local nursery or sod supplier and explain your needs and site attributes.

**Vegetative lawn alternatives.** These are very popular in climates that don't naturally support lawns. Basically, they are expanses of low-growing 1- to 4-inch-tall vegetation that can support light foot traffic. Meadows, clumping grasses and other low-growing plants are great alternatives to water-loving lawns and still offer a nice green or flowering aesthetic while saving water.

## VEGETATIVE GROUND COVERS

A lot of vegetative ground covers offer nice full coverage that requires less maintenance than lawns if the foot traffic is infrequent or a pathway is installed to navigate around it. These plants have different ways of spreading, from underground roots to clumping to above-ground branching. Ground covers usually grow from about 6 inches to 2 feet tall and can serve a variety of purposes, from growing over a slope to filling in space. Low-growing plants can be a great addition anywhere to add scale and color. Check out your local nursery, and be sure to ask about water usage, foot traffic and growing habits.

### BENEFITS OF USING GROUND COVER

- Replaces lawns in drought-stricken areas
- Is able to handle foot traffic and saves water
- Retains and reinforces an existing slope
- Helps protect and insulate soil, creating a blanket effect
- Creates dimension and habitat in the yard

# INSTALLING SOD AND CURVED EDGING

**LEVEL: BEGINNER**
**COST: $$**
**TIME COMMITMENT: 1 AFTERNOON**
**PROFESSIONALS NEEDED: NONE**
**DIMENSIONS: 18' × 20' (ABOUT 300 SQ FT IF CURVED)**

Having a green expanse of open space is inviting and versatile, so it is no wonder people love their lawns. For climates that are accommodating to lawns, wide stretches of grass can make a lot of sense to create open space. In areas that struggle with drought, maintaining a small, purposeful lawn is a more appropriate way to have open space for playing, lounging and other activities. Using sod is the quickest way to achieve a big impact, as you need to wait only about two weeks before it's ready for foot traffic. Sod is thickly planted so that it is hard for weeds to gain a foothold. A more affordable option is to spread grass seed, but then you need to control weeds, which will compete with the new grass, and it will take a bit longer to fill in. Using a decorative edging to contain the lawn is attractive and defines the space. These garden borders can be used for lawn alternatives or garden spaces in general.

You will need to order your sod a few days ahead of time for delivery or pick up from your location. Most big box stores sell it for pickup, but you'll probably get the best rates at a nursery or going directly to a sod farm. Sod is cut the day it is delivered and it is best to install it as soon as possible. Within a few hours is fine, and I've even seen it installed the next day, but it's not recommended. If you need to leave your sod out, be sure to wet it down so it doesn't dry out. Plan to hand water unless you want to install an irrigation system. Sod is an easy way to freshen up your yard almost instantly and it is not necessarily hard to install, but it is important to do it right. Skipping key steps like tilling up the soil or not watering enough for the first weeks are surefire ways to fail. This project will guide you through the basic steps so you can have a happy and healthy lawn for your family to enjoy.

## TOOLS

- Gloves
- Hose
- Pickaxe
- Rototiller (optional)
- Kneepads
- Mallet
- Leveling rake
- 2" × 4" scrap piece for screeding
- Utility knife or sod cutter
- Utility bristle brush
- Sod roller

## MATERIALS

- 1 can marking spray
- 60 linear feet or fifteen 4' pieces of Flexi Curve Scroll edging with stakes
- 1½ cubic yards amended soil (43 cu ft)
- Sod for about 300 sq ft

STEP 1: **Select the area for lawn:** Lawns do best with full sun, although many varieties do well in part shade. Place it in an area that will get plenty of use. I chose this small space in the clear of all the surrounding trees that gets six hours or more of direct sun a day. Decide whether you'd like a square or curvilinear lawn area. Squared areas are easier to lay out than curved ones. To visually see what your curves will look like, use a garden hose as a guide. Once you like the curves, mark them with marking spray.

If your climate requires irrigation, then hire a professional or DIY it. You can also hand water or set an attachment to your hose and skip adding in ground irrigation, but you must commit to watering often if needed.

STEP 2: **Select your edging:** Edging curved areas is tough if you don't have a good product. For this project, I used a decorative rubber edging called Flexi Curve Scroll, which is attached with spikes and available at most big box stores. If your soil is tough, wet down the area before installing the edging so the stakes will glide in easily. There are other, simpler, rolled plastic options on the market, but they are not as easy to install and they don't look as "finished."

STEP 3: **Secure the edging:** Trench out the border with a pickaxe. You might want to put on kneepads for the rest of the project, as you'll be kneeling quite a bit. Place the edging in the trench and hammer in the provided stakes with a mallet, turning or curving the edging as needed.

**STEP 4:** **Prepare the soil:** Start by tilling up the first 2 to 4 inches of soil with a pickaxe or a rototiller. Use a rake to pull out any clumps, broken branches, rocks or other debris. Then add 1 inch of the new amended soil and use a 2×4-inch board to screed and level the area. The area must be very even, as divots and pits will create an uneven surface and collect water.

**STEP 5:** **Mist the soil:** Mist down the soil to compact it and provide moisture to your thirsty sod, which will be in shock from being cut a few hours before.

**STEP 6:** **Lay the sod:** Lay out the sod piece by piece. I like to start in the center and run a straight line from one end to the other and then work my way out on both sides. When you start the next row, stagger the seams halfway so that no lines meet up. (Note: Position yourself to be standing on the soil rather than working on top of the sod, as shown in the photo.)

**STEP 7:** **Relevel:** Use the leveling rake to even out the soil as you go, because it will be disturbed when you are kneeling on it to install the sod. Rewet the soil if needed.

**STEP 8:** **Cut the sod:** Use a utility knife or sod cutter to make cuts as needed along the edging or while fitting pieces together. Make sure when you cut that the piece fits flat so that the roots can easily grow into the soil. Avoid cutting pieces that are too small. Whenever possible, cut one larger piece rather than scrapping together smaller ones because they dry out quickly and don't take as well.

**STEP 9:** **Brush dirt into the seams:** After all the sod is rolled out, spread some soil on the seams and use a brush to brush it in. This helps fill in any voids and keeps the edges from drying out, as they are the most vulnerable.

**STEP 10:** **Roller the sod:** Run over the new sod with a sod roller half filled with water to level it out and press it into the new soil.

**STEP 11:** **Water and wait:** Now you have an instant lawn, but be patient, you want to avoid walking on it—including your pets—for at least two weeks as the roots need to establish. Water thoroughly at least twice a day. If you're in a hot climate, avoid watering during the hottest hours of the day because water will evaporate quickly and water sitting on the grass can magnify the sun's rays and burn the vegetation. Once the lawn is established you can cut back to watering a few times a week or as needed for your area. Give it a nice mow here and there and leave the grass clippings on the lawn to help add nitrogen to the soil.

# ACKNOWLEDGMENTS

A big thank-you to my colleagues, suppliers and friends. I wouldn't have these opportunities without the help and knowledge you guys share. I am ever so grateful for your help, support and friendship.

Thanks to El Dorado Stone, which has top-notch natural and artificial stone veneers, barbecue cabinets and fireplace kits that you see in the fireplace and kitchen counter projects. Thank you to Thompson Building Materials for offering a plethora of building materials from natural stone to pavers, and a special thanks to Derek Pritchett, for lending his time and knowledge to answer all my concrete questions. To Southwest Boulder and Stone, which has more natural stone than anyone and an extremely knowledgable staff. Kelli, Andrew and Michelle, you have been a great resource for natural stone, bocce ball mix, beautiful reflective fire glass and other landscape materials. Thanks to Kevin Gallagher, my buddy at Ewing Irrigation, for constantly checking in with me and helping me with all my lighting, irrigation and random questions. To Daroll Adams and the whole crew at Beefeater Barbecues and AF Distributors, for their support and awesome line of grills and accessories. To Jim Boucher, for sharing his insight and knowledge in the world of grills. To Moon Valley Nurseries, especially Justin Virabalin and team, for being available and having an awesome selection of plants for me to build my gardens with. To Rob Mirkovic at Bravo Fuoco Pizza Ovens, whom I met at a trade show and who graciously helped me lug a copious amount of exterior furniture to my car—more important, he turned me on to accessible pizza ovens for all budgets. To Razor-Back professional tools, for providing top-grade tools and sharing a passion for well-built tools and projects. To Shelby Simmers, a creative seamstress, who made my custom-fitted cushions and helped make the bocce ball court cover. To Carl Petit at Colombia Water Gardens, for all his support over the years and for being my water feature resource. A big shout-out to Wayfair, with whom I partner from time to time, for their awesome support of what I do and helping me style the yard from their versatile collection of goods online. To Mercedes Austin at Mercury Mosaic, for the beautiful handmade tiles that I used in the mosaic potting project. Special thanks to my uncle Frank Garcia and Miramar Bobcat Inc. for always being there for me when I need to push some dirt around.

Thank you to the people who lent me their time and shared there professional opinions about landscape and home value, including John Harris at Landscape Economics LLC, Cy Carlberg, Scott Culllen RCA and Terri Dillon at Realty Executives Dillon.

Most important, thank you to my family, who have always been there for me, and are never afraid to point out my shortcomings and praise my good doings . . . I am grateful. To Mom, Dad, Jess, Lizzy, Teddy, JJ, Aunt Carmen, Uncle Frank, Alex, Nina, Jimmy and Evie, for all your DIY help on projects for this book. Thank you to my extended family over the years for their unwavering support of my crazy ideas and dreams.

To my crew and colleagues: Thank you, Maurice Temple, for your amazing talent, attention to detail, quality and crazy knowledge of anything lumber; John Serbian, for your ability to build what I need with little direction and superb creativity; Denver Henry, for reliable carpentry skills, support and for shooting hoops with me when I need a break; Tomas, Lalo, Rene and Alex, for lending your professional talents to bring my ideas to fruition; Louis Rubera, for all your hard work, being strong enough to move anything I can't and having random knowledge about everything; Navid Mostatabi at Envision Landscape Architecture, for friendship, selfless support and responding to my excessive text messages; Memo Garcia and Mike Martinez from Epic Landscapes, for being great resources and collaborators for my many crazy ideas; Blake Weyland, the only person I could convince to dig holes in exchange for rock climbing; Dylan Eastman, for beautiful photos, support and friendship; and Joe Dodds, my main photographer, for his commitment, great photos and friendship.

To Page Street Publishing, for giving me the opportunity to expand myself and share my passion between these pages. I am so grateful for all of the support and guidance I've received from your team. To Sarah Monroe and Karen Levy, particularly, for dealing with my crazy schedule. I appreciate you!

# ABOUT THE AUTHOR

**SARA BENDRICK** is a landscape designer/contractor and the host of the DIY Network's *I Hate My Yard!* She has her own design and construction business, Sarita Landscape Design, based in San Diego, California. Sara has been featured in numerous newspapers and magazines, including *HGTV Magazine* and *Everyday Home Magazine* and was on the cover of *HOSS* magazine with her fellow DIY colleagues. She writes a monthly column for *San Diego Home/Garden Lifestyles* magazine and cohosts a monthly empowerment chat with @PrettyHandyGirl called #DIYCourage. Sara is a frequent guest speaker on home improvement shows across the country and recently presented a TEDx talk about passion at her alma mater, Cal Poly State University, San Luis Obispo. She is currently filming a new pilot for the DIY Network and will be a cohost for a new landscaping show with Chris Lambton from *Yard Crashers*.

# INDEX